Colopho.

Quantum Tran
Analysis & thin.....g along
with great minds of old

As an antidote to the
C-superstition & the C-voodoo
from today

By Anne Wuyts

www.annewuyts.be
2022

The book is self-published. However, when printing on demand, there is a great temptation to tinker with the text, correct a typo, revise a sentence structure or reconsider the layout. The covers of the books are also occasionally reworked. Of course, the content remains untouched.

You are allowed to quote the new concepts (quantum transactional analysis) from this edition and incorporate them into your own work. You must mention me. That strokes my ego. Ultimately, I know that these concepts were given to me by the Field. They don't belong to me. Actually, this book belongs to everyone. That is why I invite you to build on my work, as I build on the works of my predecessors.

Cover: photo of Buddha head (internet), photoshopped in my painting, "my being" (cfr. cover of book 2).

Preface

In the preface I always refer to what we have studied so far and what we already know. What follows is a very brief summary listing the concepts specific to quantum transactional analysis (QTA). Reference is also made to the book where the content of these concepts is discussed in detail. You may need to go over a few things here and there so you know the terminology and what it's all about. The concepts used in QTA have a specific meaning and are not open to interpretation.

QTA presents a vision for those who are looking for more than just academic knowledge and for those who want to evolve. It is not an easy frame of reference and if you want to delve into it you will have to make an effort and keep your focus. Some readers will be tempted to kick QTA out and dismiss it as unscientific rubbish. Those are the ones who got stuck in the Baconian integration phase and who don't want to grow. Others relish it, get energy from it and long for more. In any case, QTA is a totally new frame of reference that is offered to people who long to individuate and who want to help building the New World, the Aquarius era.

QTA is about the evolution of man and humanity through the phases of symbiosis, separation, integration, individuation and socialization. These stages of development are passed through by individuals (Book 1) as well as by humanity as a collective (Book 3). This has been further developed in detail since book 10 (the corona chronicles) and especially in book 14 & 15.

QTA is a frame of reference that fits into the spiritual, new quantum paradigm, which assumes an intelligent, living universe, in which everything is connected to everyone, and where the hermetic starting point, "as above so below", is a law of nature. We leave behind the old materialistic, Cartesian, Darwinian, Pasteurian, Baconian, Newtonian paradigm that assumes a lifeless cosmos, built of dead building blocks and functioning like a well-oiled machine. In schools and universities, teaching is still based on this static, materialistic worldview, which has been on the rise since the Enlightenment and is based on "coincidence" and "cause-and-effect thinking" instead of "synchronicity" (book 2 & 9). The result is a quantitative science we are supposed to believe in. This science with its dogmas and creeds is amoral, and leads straight to the destruction of our planet and its inhabitants. People who believe in this science and who profess this science, I call integration people. Since the Enlightenment, here in the West at least we live in a collective integration phase, which was hijacked by the anti-God Ahriman, with all the consequences that entails. You can read about the anti-hierarchies in all books and especially in book 4 and the corona chronicles.

QTA offers a rather spiritual-esoteric conceptual framework, combining Eric Berne's transactional analysis and Rudolf Steiner's anthroposophy. Furthermore, QTA is supplemented with conceptual frameworks from philosophy (book 3), Jungian analytical psychology (book 7; 8 & 9); the Hahnemannian unitary homeopathy (books 4 & 15), and the alchemy of Paracelsus (books 15 and 16). KTA is a frame of reference that has left the Old School. It belongs to the New School and invites you to think.

QTA is also a frame of reference with great sympathy for age-old intellectual underground currents, such as those of the Manicheans, the Cathars and the Rosicrucians (book 5). They are groups composed of highly evolved individualities initiated into the ancient Hermetic Mysteries. These initiations were not always harmless and required great willpower and focus. You can read more about this in book 14. In these communities, men and women were equal and they had no private property. You could say that these were individualities that had reached the socialization stage.

QTA is a concept that invites people to go beyond the integration phase and to take people to a higher form of consciousness, a consciousness that is specific to people who individuate, a consciousness that is appropriate for the Aquarius era on the rise. It is about a different way of thinking, a thinking that is rather Michaelic and beyond Ahriman's control (book 14). We are talking here about a rather imaginative thinking, a thinking in which the heart participates and which inspires the will to immediately accomplish the good in a precarious situation (book 14).

In the evolution of mankind that began millions of years ago, we developed a material body, an etheric body and an astral body as our vehicles or body parts, with which we walk around here on earth. Now the time has come to develop a strong thinking I, so that we can merge into our higher self and finally into the World I (book 14). That I is our immortal core, which we carry with us in every incarnation and that I is the thinker in us. We are created in the image and likeness of our creator, the Logos, a thought. Our core, or I, is thought, love and morality. This core, or I-force, must continue to unfold as we let grow higher parts of beings, each time with a higher consciousness (book 14). In ancient times, people who were more advanced in their evolution were initiated in the greatest secrecy by a hierophant. Today, life itself, with its obstacles and challenges, is a path of initiation in itself. It's about maintaining your willpower and your focus, while exploring things for yourself. You take your life into your own hands and you don't let anything be imposed on you. You are free but not without obligation.

By exploring things for yourself, I mean turning away from the quantitative or objective, materialistic science based on the old paradigm with its rigid, repetitive laboratory experiments, which often victimize laboratory animals, as well as test subjects. Because it is a science that, along with politically correct thinking, is part of the indoctrination that we were taught in our upbringing. Objective science is practiced by myopic integration scientists with a tunnel vision and who specialize in the smallest possible building blocks of the whole. They by no means think holistically, they do not see the links, they do not connect dots and they think only one step ahead. They love statistics, tables, logarithms, procedures and rules, in which common sense should not participate. In addition, this "science" is sponsored by large companies and the research results are adapted to the requirements of the moneylenders. It is an amoral, materialistic science that serves the economically greedy man. And with this you suddenly have a picture of how the anti-God Ahriman has stolen the thinking of the integration man, along with his empathy and his morality.

QTA prefers phenomenological scientific research, also known as qualitative or subjective scientific research. In that context we already discussed great thinkers such as Husserl, Heidegger, Sartre (book 8), Hahnemann (book 4 & 15), Paracelsus (book 15), Jung (book 7, 8 & 9), Goethe (book 6 & 16) and Steiner (any book). Phenomenology means that each one examines things for himself. You don't believe anything. You read, study, experience, test, observe and think with your mind and hart. You use your knowledge of discernment and your moral compass to the fullest. You then come to conclusions that fit into your own frames of reference. If these frames of reference work well for understanding the world and for possibly making predictions, then they are good, usable frames of reference for you, which are not based on a belief, but on your own thinking. Then you will share your results and conclusions with other thinkers, without imposing or trying to convince, because thinkers are free people. They are free thinkers and freedom is our highest good. In that sharing of knowledge, you expand your conceptual frameworks and your perceptions approach reality more and more. This reality is just like our vehicles, both material and subtle.

QTA has its own theory of knowledge which is called quantum thinking. That's how it goes. If we want to examine reality, we run into a difficulty, because we filter this reality twice. Once through our senses and once through our script. As long as we have not fully developed our higher parts of being that go together with a higher and more spiritual consciousness, we have only five senses and with them we can only explore the material world. That is not to say that there are no other more subtle worlds or other more ethereal dimensions. Integration scientists say "there is no life on Mars". More educated people say: "in the third dimension, sensory world there is no life on Mars". And even more educated people with more sophisticated spiritual senses may well know who lives on Mars.

In addition, we filter with our script. That is to say that as children we programmed ourselves to survive in the context

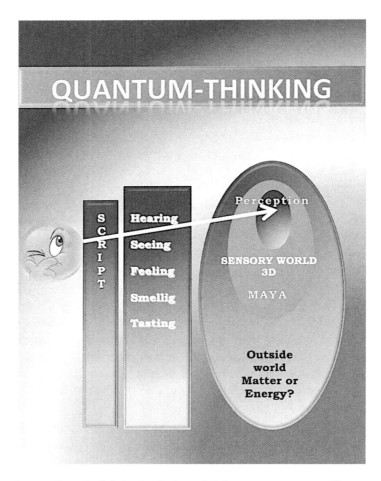

(family, cultural, historical) in which we grew up. Our script consists of all conscious and especially unconscious beliefs about ourselves and the world. Moreover our script was very malleable and susceptible to indoctrination, brainwashing, mass manipulation and mind control. So when we observe things, there are two serious filters in the way, which makes us see what we want to see and hear what we want to hear. What we ultimately notice are mere perceptions, illusions and projections. Because we simply filter out what does not fit in our script.

There are different types of scripts such as winner scripts, loser scripts, dramatic scripts and banal scripts. There are also cultural scripts, historical scripts, company scripts, family scripts, etc. The good news is that we can transform our script. We often do this in painful grieving processes, where we are close to despair and then we question everything. In such moments, nothing is self-evident anymore. Therapy can support these script-transforming processes provided it is not behavioral therapy and is not associated with suppressive chemicals such as antidepressants. Adversity can invite us to become a better and more highly developed human being. Misfortune can also make us sink even deeper into our script. From a spiritual point of view your script is the materialization of your karma and sometimes there is simply no way out of your karma and you just have to go through it, taking things as neutrally and resignedly as possible.

The script is a stubborn thing and takes away your freedom. Whoever does not transform his script will always act on auto-pilot and he will have no control over his life. Moreover, you radiate and attract what you are. You will always end up in similar situations and meet the same kind of people. With your script you create your reality and the script will repeat and confirm itself over and over. However, whoever transforms his script will create different and more desirable realities. We call that working with the field, the quantum field of zero point energy. The field always gives what you (unconsciously) ask for. Convictions always come true. Thoughts are powers. You can read all about script and script transformation in book 1.

If you do not have the books to which I refer, you can find a lot of information on my website and my blog: www.annewuyts.be; https://transvormmensiablog.wordpress.com/.

It is interesting to supplement quantum thinking with what the diligent Goethe says about it. For him, nature expresses its rich content in various ways. For each individual person, the truth reveals itself in an individual form. It conforms to the specific character of his personality. In order to discover the truth, each person projects his spiritual, most intimate experiences and at the same time the most characteristic of his personality onto the perceived world. Thus reality is colored individually. This is of course not the case with everything that can be measured, counted or weighed. Because those are mathematical truths and they are the same for everyone. However, when it comes to penetrating into the essence of things, it is experienced differently by everyone. It is of course not the case that the truth appears differently in every person, but that all the individual forms of it appearing are part of one great whole, namely the universal world of ideas. The truth speaks different languages and dialects in the interior of individual people. In every great person she speaks a language of her own, which is given only to this one personality. But it is one and the same truth that speaks.

Since the corona plandemic that started in March 2020, I have been following closely what is happening in front of and behind the scenes. You will find its outcome in the corona chronicles that start with book 10. The entire corona circus is seriously questioned and placed within the frames of reference of QTA. That is, we view what is happening from a higher consciousness, a better functioning moral compass and a way of thinking that transcends that of the average integration person. I'm not the only one, by the way, who is amazed at how stupid and gullible the masses are, as they line up again and again in long lines to be injected with deadly poison yet again.

In the corona chronicles you will also find what vaccines are and what they contain. If you are "jab-sorry", you can read what the antidotes are. These are mainly the antioxidants N-acetylcysteine and glutathione. These eliminate the graphene oxide from your system, provided you are not already connected to the network of things. They also work well in combination with vitamin D, chlorella, eating oily fish and a glass of wine. You can resist the spike proteins with vitamin C and pine needles tea. If you have been injected with ricin, a poison that produces the same symptoms as Marburg, the little sister of Ebola, ie internal and external bleeding, then according to a homeopath I know, nitricum acidum would be the appropriate remedy. I do think it is wise, if the time comes, to discuss this with your own homeopath and let him determine the dose. Moreover, we know that viruses are not pathogens. They are the consequences of an unhealthy lifestyle and a poorly functioning immune system.

Content

* Introduction

* Happy New Year

* What is really going on and what can we do?

* What about our money and what is the alternative?

* Kitesh

* Goethe 's morphology

* Sulfur Mercure Sal

* Faust

* The art of medicine of Paracelsus

* Individuation as an antidote for cancer

* February: the World Freedom Convoys, military actions in Ukraine and the Nürnberg II trials

* March: Ukraine panic replaces corona panic

Introduction

Book 16 is mainly about Paracelsus and Goethe, two thinkers who already possessed an imaginative consciousness, with which they could fathom nature in a way that far transcends the integration man of today. It is therefore not difficult to explain that these two already very advanced individualities are ridiculed, trivialized and cast aside in the present victorious and Ahriman hijacked collective integration phase. Thinking along with Goethe and Paracelsus is no easy task for those who have been raised, trained and brainwashed as an integration person. Rather, it's brain-stretching, and that's exactly the point

In addition, you get the contemporary corona news. The unnecessary, freedom-robbing measures will be suspended by spring and replaced by a terrifying threat of war in Ukraine. Vaccination deaths and damage continue to rise significantly, people are awakening more and more and taking part in mass demonstrations for freedom, peace and love, while the press only reports on the police and Soros-sponsored Antifa riots. The question remains how quickly they will make the syringe mandatory for everyone, the (sham) debates about this are being held. Children from 5 years old are already vaccinated and the poor little victims fall like flies. We are talking about the plans of the globalists and how we can counteract this through far-reaching decentralization. Thus we tell about some parallel societies in the making. There is Vrijland with its own currency: the Vrijduit, which is based on the already existing Lets. LETS stands for 'local exchange trading system' and is already applied throughout Flanders. There is also Bob De Wit's society 4.0.

When I think further about that famous Vrijduit (free money), it must be a currency not based on the gold standard, but on human activity. So the harder people work, the more money comes into circulation and a lot of money in circulation creates wealth. So the more people work, the richer people get and that makes sense. It would therefore be a coin that in no way belongs to a bank or state or any other institution and which you cannot print till it is broken and thus, totally worthless. If you don't lend free money at an interest rate, it can't devalue, because then you don't create money out of thin air. This is actually genius. In addition, the state cannot trace this money or raise taxes on it. The question is whether this will become a digital currency, or will it be shaped differently.

We also talk about how the West, with real contempt for death, is heading for an armed conflict with Russia. The corona scam can no longer last and mega-inflation is unstoppable. A third world war could divert attention. But the destruction of Russia would mean a real disaster for the development of humanity. The Russian language belongs to the spirit-self (or manas), a more highly developed part of being associated with the imaginative consciousness. We remember from book 14 that when the sentient soul has been released by the human I from the subjectivity of the feelings of sympathy and antipathy and from the desire life of the astral body and is raised to an objectively pure spiritual experience, the astral body is transformed into spirit self by the action of the I. This spirit self as a more highly evolved being part should be fully unfolded in the sixth post-Atlantean civilizational period, also called the Aquarius age. The Russian folk spirit is preparing this era. The heyday of this future sixth post-Atlantic cultural period should take place in Russia. That is why there will also be written about the Russians, their folk soul and their grail legend in the chapter about Kitesh.

Other breaking news is that of the "Freedom Convoy 2022". Canadian truckers crossing the US border are required to be vaccinated on 15/1/22. The drivers indicated that they did not agree with this, after which Trudeau called them a marginal minority with unacceptable ideas. The truckers felt offended by this and with a convoy of thousands they travel from Ontario to Ottawa in order to take back their freedom. The spark is passing and millions of people brave the cold to participate in this manifestation. Temperatures in Canada are currently around minus thirty degrees.

The emphasis is on making it a peaceful event and on all sides the truckers are provoked to violence so that they can be discredited. Because the fact is that the mainstream press only reports on that really violent small marginal group with unacceptable ideas, which is often also sponsored by the government itself.

Meanwhile, freedom convoys are on their way all over the world. This book gives an account of their adventures. They encourage each other in difficult times, where they are challenged, bullied, arrested, molested and bombarded with EMF weapons by the police, their own army and NWO soldiers. Their slogan is "HOLD THE LINE".

Finally, the Nürnberg II trials will start on 5/2/22, under the telling name "Grand Jury - the court of public opinion". In this work you get an account of the progress of the process of the people, by the people and for the people. Actually, it is all a big resumption of what you could already read in the Corona chronicles. You can see it as a repetition and a deepening of what has already been mentioned. The intent of the whole process is to inform people about what is really going on, with evidence and testimonials from real, independent experts. I am already part of the jury. These processes are spread over six days. Each day deals with a specific topic, namely: the geopolitical background; the fake PCR tests; the injections; financial destruction and eugenics. Unfortunately the last session has been removed from the internet and I have not been able to see it.

My ambition in writing this book is once again to add a higher, spiritual dimension to the events we are now experiencing and that are destroying many people. On the other hand, beautiful things happen, because the conscious and awakened people are waging a tremendous non-violent struggle. They remain peaceful, worthy, polite and correct at all times. Sarcasm is allowed

Happy New Year

The Netherlands go into Lockdown against the "contagious omikron variant" from 19/12/21. It is about a common cold that does not kill anyone. Now that all non-essential shops in the Netherlands remain closed, the Dutch are shopping en masse in Belgium, much to the delight of Belgian shopkeepers. Antwerp also welcomed a lot of northern neighbors this weekend, but don't worry, Antwerp mayor Bart De Wever says laconically "Wir schaffen das". On facebook we find the following cartoon.

Lieve Mark,

Wat **goed** zeg dat je de Nederlandse zelfstandigen **te schijten** zet en onze Belgische winkels een mooi cadeau geeft. En dat **voor een snotvalling** met amper doden. Stond dat ook in het boekje van Klaus? Houden zo!!! Lockdown forever!

Dank je wel alvast! Groetjes van bij ons!

Dear Mark, it is a good thing you shitting on the Dutch self-employed and give our Belgian stores a nice gift. And that for a common cold. Was that also in Klaus' book? Keep it up!!! Lockdown forever. Thank you very much and greetings from us.

A week before Christmas, we got the laughter again because virologist Steven Van Gucht advised everyone to celebrate

Christmas under the extractor fan. Jokes and cartoons about this were once again skyrocketing.

Corona nativity scene, including extractor hood, order now, exclusive discount for sheeple.

In vrtNWS of 28/12/21 it is about an analysis of the coordinating body for threat analysis (OCAD) that comes to the following conclusion. The handling of the corona crisis has led to social disruption, economic malaise and feelings of insecurity. This is fertile ground for polarization and extremist ideologies. But the corona-critical counter-movement, which emerged en masse during the latest demonstrations against the Covid Save Ticket, does not in any way consist of extreme right-wing individuals. The chanted mantras "Love and connection" and "We exclude no one" indicate that everyone is welcomed with open arms, including the far right. OCAD advises to listen to the criticism of the measures. It's nice that the wappies and conspiracy theorists are finally being taken a bit more seriously.

In vrtNWS of 29/12/21 we read that the Council of State suspended last week's decision of the consultation committee to close the cultural sector for being disproportionate and unmotivated. Political scientist Carl Devos speaks of arbitrariness, a lack of leadership and a lack of vision. Wetstraat watcher Ivan De Vadder talks about a political cacophony, because politicians openly disagree with each other about the measures taken. Anyway, theaters, concert halls and cinemas are reopening, at least for the vaccinated, while the administrators of our country are starting to suffer more and more from loss of face. It is good that the press is once again making some more critical voices about the crazy game that calls itself government.

But you won't laugh when you read what top economist Martin Armstrong predicts (xandernieuws.net, 27/12). 2022 will be the year in which the reckoning of years of failing financial and economic policy of the EU will begin. We are dealing with an enormous economic crisis, as a result of the sovereign debt crisis. In Europe and the US governments keep borrowing money with no intention of ever repaying it. We are not dealing with a simple hyperinflation, because that implies that the currency will still survive. The currency (the euro and the dollar) will not survive this, with the result that our prosperity will receive major blows. There will never be a return to normal. Our civilization is about to collapse and if we don't say "no" en masse to the WEF, the great reset will be jammed down our throats much faster than we think. (In book 15 you can read more about the economic and financial situation we are heading for and what the causes are).

The Netherlands has a new government, cabinet Rutte 4. The Dutch resistance speaks of Schwab1. WEF puppet Sigrid Kaag gets finances. It is said that she will soon be allowed to prepare the transition to the Central Bank Digital Currency (more on this in book 15). Amsterdam alderman Eric van der Burg becomes State Secretary for Asylum and Immigration. His motto is "the more asylum seekers the better", and with that he is completely behind the Kalergi plan, which aims to disrupt Western countries by installing the so-called multicultural (European) state, which mainly consists of foreign criminals. Anyway, the cards are shuffled and dealt out and every Bilderberger gets a nice job, with which he is supposed to roll out the NWO. (Niburu 1/1/22).

We read on the same day about the first case of flurona (flu and corona at the same time) in Israel. Come on, we have not known the flu for two years and now the flu is making its way back together with corona. It is hilarious.

We read further in Niburu of 3/1/22 that the excess mortality in the last two months tends to 40% and that it concerns working people between 18 and 64 years. This is reported by, among others, some insurance companies in the US. The same news is confirmed in Xander News of the same day. It would be about vaccine deaths. Large sums of money must also be paid to those who have suffered vaccine damage and are disabled for the rest of their lives. Xander News goes one step further and refers to the military intelligence site Deagel, where it is predicted that the population in the US and Europe will decrease by one to two thirds by 2025. A prediction or a deliberately executed plan, the author wonders.

In New Zealand (Niburu of 4/1/22) the lives of useless eaters, who have less than six months to live, will be ended with active euthanasia. An article was also devoted to this in Xander News of 30/12/21.

On 4/1/22 we also read about the anti-corona & lock down demonstration in Amsterdam and the shameful police action there. A group of "cops" with strange decals on their sleeves attacked a group of veterans. The author wonders whether this could be the European Gendarmerie Force (Eurogendfor), a multinational cooperation of police forces with military status. Their main task would be to suppress revolts.

On 7/1/22 we watch David Icke's podcast where he laughs at the Cabal and the people who are giving their world away to these retarded morons. For crazy are those of the Cabal for sure and stupid too. They suffer from an anxiety disorder or more specifically an obsessive compulsive disorder, resulting in compulsive behavior. Everything has to be perfect, clean and robotic and there is no room for disorder, playfulness and creativity. They are control freaks, which means that they want to mask their fears and insecurities. Their strategy is to frighten the population. As an antidote, Icke recommends laughing at them. Then you reverse the roles. Moreover, if you look at the mass hysteria of the past two years and how grown people followed the most absurd measures out of fear, it is indeed hilarious. It is as if those of the Cabal are imposing their own compulsive behavior on the population. We think of constantly washing your hands, wearing mouth masks, not having physical contact, staying indoors, etc.

On the other hand, there are rumors that the planned epidemic is coming to an end. Denmark will stop all corona voodoo from February 1. They go back to normal. Boris Johnson also wants to stop the whole nonsense in England. At the end of January, the WHO starts to think very carefully about declaring the planned epidemic finished. Sixty percent of Europeans have been vaccinated and the many infections with the omecron variant are said to have contributed to herd immunity. Corona would be endemic controllable from now on, just like a normal flu. Well, by now we know that the Cabal's give us some hope every now and then and then strike hard again. And yes, from 28/1, Belgium will go into code red with stricter measures. Omecron would have mutated to a new subtype and virologist Steven Van Gucht predicts a new peak within two weeks. In the Netherlands, people are carefully crawling out of the strict lockdown. The QR code will of course still apply.

The mega-inflation is unstoppable, the corona scam is no longer standing and other diversions are apparently being prepared. Because yes, there must be deaths and many. Moreover, chaos is indispensable, in order to later burden the population with the NWO as an acceptable alternative.

According to some, such as top economist Martin Armstrong, we can think of an impending WWIII with Russia. Europe is bankrupt and Russia as a superpower is seriously in the way of Schwab's "great reset" and his "build back better". They certainly don't want to participate. The West is deeply provoking Putin and tensions around Ukraine are running high. We consult various articles in Xander Nieuws, between 9/1/22 and the end of January, and we also consult the regular press. So, we read that the Kremlin asks NATO not to turn Ukraine into a military NATO missile base, from which Moscow and an important military installation can be destroyed within minutes. All Russia asks is a little bit of respect and a guarantee that Ukraine will never join NATO. The answer was a resounding "no". Putin then assembled a large force near Ukraine. In Brussels, they think that they can win a war with Russia and that the Kremlin will not dare to use nuclear weapons. Russia is probably aware that Europe and the US are out for war and Russia will have realized by now that the governments in the west are made up of untrustworthy, lying bandits. Moreover, the Russians can survive a nuclear war more easily than the Europeans. Not only they are about ten to twenty years ahead of the US/EU/NATO militarily, they also have a subterranean facility in the Ural Mountains, Mount Yamantau, with enormous reserves, where tens of millions of people after a nuclear apocalypse can survive for tens of years. In 2021, they held a successful exercise that brought 40 million people into these underground installations in no time.

Anyway, thanks to the US/NATO, the talks with Russia failed on 10/1/22 in Geneva. Meetings held later also fizzled out. Meanwhile, Russia is moving large numbers of troops and materials to its borders. The US is launching a life-threatening provocation with a nuclear submarine and two carrier strike groups a short distance from Russia. On 14/1/22 a Russian submarine with sixteen Bulava missiles surfaced off the American coast (Virginia). With that, all major US cities can be reduced to nuclear ash within minutes. The British send troops to Ukraine and the Russians withdraw from the OSCE (Organization for Security and Co-operation in Europe) consultation. Russian Deputy Foreign Minister Groushko said he did not take NATO's "peaceful intentions" seriously. Europe threatens Russia to cut Europe off their cheap gas in February. The result is that we are forced to buy the much more expensive

American LNG. Moreover, the Americans do not have enough gas for us. This will only increase inflation and (energy) poverty in Europe, resulting in possible popular uprisings. And that's exactly what plays into the hands of the Davos mafia and their great reset.

NATO's military infrastructure is closing in on Russia's borders and Russia feels that its national security is increasingly being jeopardized. Russia is thus preparing for an armed conflict and that is exactly what the rogue governments in Europe and the US want. The danger is that when Russia feels too much cornered, it will defend itself by suddenly lashing out with a massive nuclear blow, which completely paralyzes the West and sends it back to the Stone Age.

Another serious American provocation was to violate Russian airspace with a military-commanded cargo plane belonging to National Airlines, which had just delivered a load of ammunition to Kiev. Fortunately, Russia did not fall into the trap and did not shoot the plane out of the sky. However, the Kremlin did show their force by having a Su-57 stealth fighter fly over Kiev completely out of nowhere and then make it disappear into thin air.

Meanwhile, the US, Germany, the UK and Australia are repatriating their diplomats and their families from Ukraine. If you read the mainstream newspapers on it, they tell that the great provocateur is Russia. They pretend that Putin holds the key to peace or war. Putin would like to invade Ukraine and the west is now supplying large-scale weapons to Ukraine so that they can defend themselves against Russia. So, dear people, put on your seat belts, because after the corona scam, we can expect an even more dangerous and bumpy journey, because who knows, we might end up in a mass-destroying WWIII.

On January 27, we hear from several alternative news stations (including Niburu and Stichting Vaccinvrij) about the "Freedom Convoy 2022". It's about the truckers' uprising in Canada. Justin Trudeau, an equally fanatical Young Global WEF leader as our unelected Prime Minister De Croo, has, like Canada and New Zealand, transformed his country into a fascist state in no time. Now the syringe will be mandatory for every truck driver crossing the border into or from the US. The truckers are teaming up and will leave on Sunday 23/1/22 in a huge convoy from Vancouver to Ottawa where they will arrive on Saturday (29/1/22). It is a 70 km journey and they will be on the road for a week. 23/1/22 was also the date of a mass demonstration in Brussels in which it is said that 500,000 demonstrators from all over Europe took part and which, thanks to Antifa, has turned into riots. So it is a historic day.

As you can see in the picture it is freezing cold in Canada. In Toronto, the mercury drops to minus 27° and in Ottawa to minus 31°. An estimated 50,000 truckers and one to two million other Canadians brave this cold to protest. The Canadians are sick and tired of Liberal Communist dictator Justin Trudeau and his government.

The plan is to surround the parliament building and the entire city center with thousands of trucks until Trudeau resigns and all vaccination obligations are lifted. Elsewhere we read that the aim is to imprison the Trudeau government, abolish the parliamentary system, cut ties with the British royal family and install a new government supported by the people and the rights of the first nation (original Indian population). There is a legal team that has determined that it is legal to overthrow a government that is causing so much harm to the population.

The truckers want to do this without violence and expect the army to stand aside.

This also triggers something in the population that awakens from its hypnosis. About 1.4 million people are said to be on their way to Ottawa. More trucks are arriving from all corners and holes and long lines of truckers are also leaving from the US to Canada to support the population there. They effortlessly cross the border with about 12,000 trucks, which could indicate that they have the customs officers on their side. Meanwhile, the head of the convoy has grown to 100 km and it takes an hour and a half before the procession has passed. The world record convoy took place in Egypt and it involved a convoy of almost five miles which corresponds to about eight km and there were 480 trucks. In Canada, about 50,000 trucks would participate, add the American trucks and that's 62,000. Despite the fact that the truckers and their organizer and spokesman Jason LaFace are talking about a peaceful manifestation, those on the other side, as Fuellmich calls them, are genuinely scared. The people are furious and they fear that the truckers will ram into parliament and that many WEF-minded politicians will be lynched. I learned via telegram that a whistleblower from the Trudeau administration is informing that the government has allocated $45 million to Antifa so that they will cause massive violence. People are urged not to participate in the violence and to film the troublemakers as much as possible.

In the meantime (28/1/22) a call has been placed for a European convoy towards Brussels. The truckers of the Netherlands are busy organizing themselves. In Canada, the parliament is surrounded and the police consider Ottawa a large parking place.

The mainstream press including HLN minimizes the issue and denies the large number of participants in the convoy. Like Trudeau, they are talking about a small minority of fringe with objectionable ideas. The Canadian government says it will stand its ground and not give in to the truckers' demands. Trudeau and his family are accommodated in a safe house, the official version is that he is in quarantine because one of his children tested positive. In an interview he states that he has no symptoms and that he is feeling fine.

Xander News reports further on the possible approaching war with Russia. The economist Armstrong believes that the West desperately needs that war and is doing everything it can to lure Russia out of its shell. The Covid Hoax can no longer last and is coming to an end. The resistance continues to grow and is now fueled by the massive peace caravan to Ottawa. Moreover, Biden is an unmitigated disaster. But what they are not counting on in the West is concerted action between Russia and China. China and Russia are economically linked, and if Moscow gets sanctions, Beijing will be hit too. Then there are the US-China clashes about Taiwan and the US Navy's continued provocations in the South China Sea. It is to be expected that, when it comes to this, both countries will not be content with a few restrictive actions. Huge, sudden and possibly nuclear surprise attacks are more likely to be launched, leaving the aggressive and arrogant West to give up for good.

What is really going on and what can we do?

On 6/1/22 there is an interview with Reiner Fuellmich on rumble.com with the title: Dr Reiner Fuellmich - update on Nuremberg 2.0. It's a nearly one-hour podcast, and much of what David Icke has been writing and saying for thirty years is reflected in Fuellmich's conclusions. Now Fuellmich has the evidence in his hands and he will indeed start the Nuremberg II trials, much coveted by the Resistance, via Lifestream and the people will act as jury. I summarize what he says and as you will see it is broadly a repetition of what has already been mentioned in the Corona Chronicles so far.

Fuellmich was fully on board with the media until 20/7/20, only then did it dawn on him that something was not right and he started an investigation committee. Meanwhile, it's clear that what Austin Fitts calls "Mr. Global" (book 15) is rolling out an agenda and they've been doing it for thirty years. They have trained many politicians and placed them in key positions, such as Merkel, Makron, Trudeau and others. In the meantime, it is clear that the whole deliberately set up corona plan with all its measures is not so much about making money, but about genocide. It is one great crime against humanity.

He then goes back to the 2009 swine flu hoax where the same protagonists were at work. The result was then also a massive vaccination of the population and especially in Scandinavia. A lot of young people got narcolepsy as a result of the syringe (book 11). Fuellmich names the culprits, including Drosten (the German Van Ranst), who created the fake PCR tests and who can lie just as well as Neil Ferguson in England.

Reference is made to Dr Mike Yeadon, ex-vice president and chief scientist at Pfizer, who warned humanity about the evil and dangerous vaccine. According to Yeadon, it's not about health, it's about chipping humanity. There is also a video where Yeadon shows Pfizer, Moderna and Johnson & Johnson trying out lethal doses in their gene-editing syringes. If you follow the lot numbers, you can see which doses are fatal. Other shots are not immediately fatal, but they do destroy your immune system, so that you can become seriously ill and die in the long run. In fact, if your immune system is no longer working, you are suffering from AIDS. The deadly shots are taken in turns by Pfizer, Moderna and Johnson & Johnson. This news is confirmed by the Niburu article of 5/1/22. You can also see a video of Dr. Jane Ruby talking to Stew Peters, where she explains that in addition to the well-known mRNA syringes, there are also syringes that are poisonous to extremely deadly. The codes on the batches allow them to keep track of who has had which syringe and what the consequences are. It's about studying how to let as many people die as possible without alarming the masses. This was already mentioned in the corona chronicles when we talked about David Icke. It is clearly about premeditated mass murder and it will be the central piece in the international process that is likely to start in a few weeks. Gates, Drosten, Fauci and Tedros will be on the dock.

Fuellmich says the several hundred or thousands of people behind this aren't in it for the money, because they own almost everything. They stole all of that from us. They use that money to bribe accomplices. They also extort people. Fuellmich thinks that ritual child abuse plays a major role in extortion. There are victims who now pose as whistleblowers and who approach Fuellmich. Fuellmich knew it existed because he had already legally represented a number of victims in the past. But the whole thing is probably much bigger than we think. The necessary evidence is still lacking to make it public in its entirety.

Ultimately, it is a major psychological operation, which has been prepared for at least thirty years and in which panic is mainly used as a weapon. For example, they make children feel responsible for the death of their grandparents, if they do not follow the absurd measures carefully. The people behind this, which is the Davos mobster, are psychopaths and sociopaths who hold a lot of puppet-strings in their hands. And although they are not interested in money, the financial mafia such as BlackRock and Vanguard are behind this (book 15). They own almost everything on this planet.

In 2008-9, the entire financial complex was on the brink of collapse. Then they started printing a lot of money. In September 2019, the entire banking system was about to explode again. But they wanted it to implode their way. If not, the Davos cabal would be exposed too soon. The corona plandemia has been put into the world purely as a diversionary manoeuvre. That had to be done quickly and besides the fact that most of them are stupid as hell, that makes that they made a lot of mistakes.

The big problem was that no one died from corona. They didn't have enough corpses and they needed them urgently because they wanted to be able to test their new drugs. That is why they asked Drosten to come up with those fake PCR tests. It is now a fact that asymptomatic infections do not exist. Yet they made everyone afraid of everyone. And the intent was to make people so mellow that they would do anything to regain their freedom, even to consent to the deadly syringes.

The cabal wants to enslave those who survive all this. They will be microchipped and monitored. Some talk about a depleted population of 500 million, but Fuellmich doesn't know that. He has no evidence for this. He also says that no one besides Big Pharma, knows what is in those syringes. What he does know is that as far as the Great Reset is concerned, they will start with Europe. Whether that will succeed is the question, because people are waking up en masse and they are taking to the streets with tens of thousands. This is happening everywhere, especially in Eastern Europe. Also, in the meantime, everyone knows someone who died from the vaccine or suffered serious damage. There is also a 40% excess mortality which is huge and many are starting to make the link to the jab. You can no longer sweep that under the rock.

Many people talk about nuremberg 2.0 and are looking forward to it. They want lawyers and scientists who state the facts and they also want a legal platform to safely oppose. Real lawyers, real judges and real witnesses will participate. The real jury will consist of the viewers. On the dock will be the puppets Gates, Tedros, Drosten and Fauci. It is especially essential to expose the fake PCR tests, because then our opponents will no longer have a leg to stand on. But most important of all, the people will be fully informed by real experts. And often these are experts who have worked for the "other side" for a long time and who know what is really going on. There are also many politicians who have joined our ranks. And besides the deliberately planned mass murder there also is the willful destruction of our economy and the deliberate destruction of our health.

These processes will not be conducted within the system, but outside it. We will show the people that we do not need a system that has been horribly corrupted. Overall, alternative courts are being set up because the system is rotten through and through. This also applies to the economic system and the education system. We have to break free from the multinationals and their puppets. We urgently need to decentralize. These regional systems can, of course, interconnect. This is how we need to restore our democracy, because, ultimately, the people on the dock were never elected by the people.

It is also very important that the whole process does not end in violence, because that is exactly what they want. We must remain peaceful at all costs and focus on what we can do regionally. We fight on three levels. The first level is education. We need to get the truth out and expose the 1% with their wrongdoing. Then there is the legal way which also serves to reveal everything and then there is the spiritual way. This certainly does not mean organized religion, because all they want is power (book 2).

All people who consciously disagree with the corona policy feel spiritually connected. They are on the same wavelength. There is clearly a spiritual force that helps us. We are protected by high spiritual entities, says Fuellmich. He feels that. And speaking of that spiritual network, Fuellmich refers to our Mattias Desmet who talks about mass crowd formation and mass hypnosis. Thirty percent of the population is hopelessly lost as a result of that. They believe the narrative and do as they are told. But forty percent have doubts and we can awaken them with the right information. Seventy percent awakened people is more than enough to skip the critical mass. The vaccinees who suffered damage and are now considered unvaccinated because they refuse the third shot are fellow combatants that should not be underestimated. Moreover, there are many more unvaccinated than they say. They lie. In Germany probably 40% is not vaccinated. In the US, only 50% to 55% would be vaccinated. Furthermore, caregivers are leaving their jobs en masse, which will lead to a shutdown of the entire healthcare system. Alternative unions are now being formed everywhere to protect unvaccinated healthcare workers.

Ultimately, the Cabal's will pay a heavy price if we take everything from them and build a beautiful new world with it. Fuellmich calls this the Great Spiritual Reckoning. The mafiosi who will survive all this, will surely end up in jail when the time comes.

In Belgium too, people are working on a new world with alternative healthcare and alternative schools. For that I go back to a podcast of rebelsonly where you can watch an interview with the now-suspended homeopath Kris Gaublomme by Elke Vermeire, nutritionist. They both focus on strengthening the immune system. Gaublomme is a doctor and worked in a group practice. However, he found that he could not sufficiently help chronic patients and patients with depression. In utter despair, he referred them to a homeopath. The results were so amazing that he sent almost all of his patients to the homeopath and didn't have a penny left. The alternative was to study homeopathy himself. In the meantime he only practices classical homeopathy (books 4 & 15) and it is his mission to make himself completely otiose as a healer.

Gaublomme has studied what vaccinations are and what they cause. Of course, this was not discussed in his training as a doctor and most patients know nothing about vaccination damage. In 1991 he set up a working group on the prevention of vaccination damage, which resulted in a non-profit association and they published a magazine. All articles in it are scientifically substantiated. For example, there is a correlation between the measles-mumps vaccine and autism, which has been scientifically proven. More information can be found on vaccinatieschade.be.

Now more and more doctors are standing up to the corona measures, because they are completely unscientific and ineffective. The Order of Physicians goes to great lengths to intimidate and exclude these doctors. But whoever follows his moral compass cannot be silenced. This also applies to Gaublomme. He is now retired and in the meantime he has another project called "Vrijland" (freeland). It is about establishing a free, autonomous, parallel society with a group of conscious and awake people. Meanwhile there are five hundred members. They are all soul mates, who are on the same wavelength and are committed to a better society. In this society autonomy, freedom, equality, respect, non-violence, health, ecology, connection and basic democracy are of paramount importance. The idea is to become self-sufficient in energy, nutrition and health. Education is called "EduCreation". Alternative forms of housing are also being considered. All these items are worked out in different working groups that meet on a regular basis and keep each other informed of their progress. It's a close-knit group of true friends who are there for each other.

Gaublomme thinks that difficult times will come and that a totalitarian state will want to manifest itself. However, totalitarian regimes are generally short-lived and when all is over, a new and better society will rise from the ashes. We can't go back to the old normal, it doesn't exist anymore. There is the chaos of now and the new world that will grow out of it. It will become a spiritual world, because what you see nowadays is that people who have never engaged in spirituality are open to it. The vibration level is increasing noticeably and that is unstoppable.

An alternative health care system will also be established with the suspended doctors and the unvaccinated health care providers who are excluded from the regular system. This will also result in a non-profit organization called "Samenzorg" (together-care). Initially, you will be able to call a platform with a request for help, such as "I am looking for a dentist who does not ask for a QR code." You will then be referred to the appropriate care provider who lives in your area. If you want to participate, there are a number of conditions. No discrimination between jabbed and no-jabbed will be allowed. Healthcare providers should be able to work holistically. And above all, self-reliance will have to be strived for. The intention is that people do not become dependent on care providers. Education for a healthy lifestyle will play a major role in this. In the meantime, there are an unimaginable number of people who want to participate in this. There are already more than two thousand candidates. You could say that the New World is already here. The website is Samenzorg.nu

Another initiative for regionalization is Prof. De Wit's society-4th. We will inform ourselves at society4th.org. In this society, the interests of the citizens are central. Technological developments play a role here in terms of energy, food, health and education. There are nine regional domains.

* Democracy: Because the scale of the future society is the region, a different democratic process for decision-making is needed. Companies own themselves. There are no outside shareholders. They are cooperative enterprises with full legal capacity and the members are entrepreneurs and citizens in the region. Blockchain technology is used to facilitate.

* Regional economy: the money thus remains largely in the regions and that stimulates local production and consumption.

* Payment and banking with local money and more specifically local crypto money, based on blockchain technology.

* A regional digital infrastructure ensures that ownership of the data is preserved. Thus, an autonomous, regional, decentralized network can be built as well as an autonomous regional internet.

* Regional utilities for water and energy are indispensable. We are talking about solar and wind energy here. Water extraction can be accommodated in a foundation or cooperative.

* Health starts with prevention, i.e. proper nutrition, exercise, relaxation. Man's relationship with nature must be restored. Healthcare should not be based on a revenue model. People's health must be paramount. Alternative and natural treatment methods should also be given a place.

* Local, healthy and sustainable food, which is produced in regional cooperatives, has a place alongside larger-scale production on fertile land, where stocks are also built up.

* New initiatives are being developed regarding housing. More will be shared, such as bicycles, cars,... .

* Education will no longer focus solely on the labor market. Emotional intelligence, learning to think critically, communication, collaboration, social skills and creative thinking deserve a prominent place in education. Young people should learn to discover what their talents are and should be given the opportunity to develop their talents. Schools are not disconnected from society, they are an integrated part of it.

More on Bob de Wit 's society 4.0, you can find in book 13.

What about our money and what is the alternative?

In book 15 we already explored what is going on with our money. Reading it can give you a lot of clarity. The conclusion is that money is no longer worth anything and that we are facing massive hyperinflation. The entire corona crisis serves to obtain a postponement and to switch to an NWO with a digital currency. Yet it remains a difficult and complicated matter.

Here I discuss a movie called "Money, banks and Michel van Peel". Michel van Peel is a stand up comedian, who mainly jokes about last year's current affairs. He apparently figures things out thoroughly and explains the matter in a very simple and funny way. But actually it invites more to cry. He starts with fractional banking. If you bring 100€ to the bank, they can lend that 100€. The borrowers pay back the money with interest and that's how the banks make money. That seems logical. But, the question is: "where does that interest come from?" Because that money was really not there. Now it is true that it is due to printing money. That way you always create more debt than there is money in the world. That is why we have a budget deficit. The system is based on economic growth. In that way, the taxes of the future must be sufficient to pay the interest on the current debts. It seems that the government is borrowing money to build one fiscal pit, filling another one with it. Yet, up to now, wealth has been created in this way, by lending money that did actually not exist.

Now it is the case that the bank, of the 100 € that you have put in it, only really needs 1% in cash to be able to lend that 100 €. The reserve coefficient in the eurozone is therefore 1%. The other 99% is used for mortgages, debt and credit. If 1% of the capital were demanded back by the people, the whole system would collapse. That is why banks make it so difficult if you want to withdraw a large sum of cash.

Van Peel then refers to the Greek situations just before the corona crisis. You could only withdraw € 20 per day in cash. The system then continues to run for a while because no one requests their money. In Cyprus in 2011, there was a similar situation. One night, 10% of each savings account was stolen. The next morning the doors opened and the banks were healthy again.

In 1971 they got off the gold standard and then they started printing money. The more money is printed the less it is worth, the less money is in circulation, the more it is worth. In March 2020, there was so much money in circulation that its value was close to zero. Then they have put everyone in lock-down and paid them out because, the money was literally printed to pieces. On the other hand, the money in the lock-down was kept, it was not spent. That slowed inflation for a while. A year later we are again facing inflation and the prices of gas and electricity are skyrocketing.

Meanwhile, the value of the euro against the dollar is falling. I.e. that more euros are printed than dollars. If no euros had been printed, the dollar would now be worthless compared to the euro. On 4/1/22, according to De Tijd, Belgian savings will lose 22 billion euros in purchasing power. The same day it is stated in De Standaard that Erdogan has stuck with 80% inflation. Turkey is already experiencing hyperinflation. Savings are worth just as much as toilet paper.

He then talks about the digital euro. That's programmable money. And that means that from its launch, your "old" money no longer works. Money will be given an expiration date, within which it must be spent. And that to keep the economy going. In addition, the government has access to your money and your money can be withheld as a punitive measure. Furthermore, the government can determine on what you can and may spend your money. In July 2021 it was decided to start with the digital euro. This will be linked to your QR code. That way they always know where you are and what you're buying. For example, if you buy too many cigarettes, they can increase your health insurance contribution, if you go to the gas station too much, your CO_2 tax will rise. You can also print a digital euro in peaces, so to speak. In other words the money is dying like it did a hundred years ago. Ultimately, they want to get rid of the cash. Because then they have full control over every transaction. Specialists recommend investing in valuable as-sets, such as precious metals and crypto coins, that a bank or government cannot take away. If people's confidence in money disappears, they will invest in it. Bitcoin is recommended be-cause it is the fastest horse in the race. It's new and young. It will win on the fiat money. Bitcoin is a decentralized currency. There are a maximum of 21 million bitcoins and bitcoins be-come scarcer every four years. It is basically the digital version of gold. Gold will always become scarcer. You can't keep mining it forever. Bitcoin will also always become scarcer. Central banks own a lot of gold and they really won't break the price of gold.

Now we see that large companies such as Tesla and Paypall are investing in bitcoin. Tesla buys one and a half billion bitcoins and in the meantime bitcoin has reached a new record level. It is now worth $44,000. Few people are involved with bitcoin (2% of the world population). Van Peel still thinks bitcoin is dange-rous and recommends investing in precious metals.

Van Peel then talks about inflation. The index goes up by 2.3% and that is not even enough to pay 1/5 of what the electricity is become more expensive. Then we move on to how the hyper-inflation in Venezuela was solved. In 2018, prices have doubled every month for the last nine months. In August the inflation rate was 80,000%. That was a record for Latin America at the time, and experts predicted that inflation could reach 300,000 to 400,000% that year. The government wanted to solve this by introducing a new digital currency (the petro) to replace the old currency (the bolivar). The new and the old coins were used in parallel for a while and then the old notes (bolivar) were with-drawn from circulation. But the petro has no value and the government has also "printed" this coin to peaces. And then something else happened. Suddenly the entire population had knowledge of crypto coins. Everyone had to install an app on their mobile phone to be able to pay with the petro. As a result, the people of Venezuela meanwhile pay with the dash, an un-traceable private currency, over which the government has no control. The government has absolutely no control over their assets and can no longer raise taxes. The people of Venezuela are no longer paying for a rogue government. The government no longer has public money to spend on war material, for example. Former government services are now run by private companies, which you pay directly. Those who have children help to pay for schools, those who are childless do not. Those who use the roads pay for it, etc. Well, that is certainly a road to follow, if there are enough of us.

In Xander News of 7/1/22 you can read about the major bailout of the banks that took place at the end of 2019 and cost taxpayers €4 trillion. In the US, they spent $4.5 trillion to pump into the mega-banks. This "emergency loan" operation lasted until July 2020. In 2008, the bailouts cost $3.1 trillion, up from $29 trillion by July 2010. We find the same information in Niburu of 6/1/22. Both websites get this information from the American website "Wallstreet Parade". Investigative journalists take a look at what's really happening in the murky world of finance on Wall Street. The bottom line is that the entire financial system had collapsed once again and that the corona pandemic was the perfect cover to obscure the bailout of the big banks. We also read which banks were kept on their feet: JP Morgan Chase, Goldman Sachs and citigroup. These are the same banks that were not allowed to crash in 2008, because otherwise the entire financial system would collapse. The owners of these banks are the same as the Federal Reserve (FED) and the New York FED.

Kitesh

In this chapter I will talk about the Russian grail legend, or the Kitesh myth and the Russian folk soul. Because, as already mentioned in the introduction, according to the anthroposophical frame of reference, the next phase in human development, or the Age of Aquarius, will take place in Russia. There the socialization phase will have to become a fact and the spirit self will descend into the human souls and come to full maturity. That brings with it a higher consciousness, the imaginative consciousness.

The legend tells that Kitesh, the invisible city, had no fortress walls and that the people who went on their spiritual path and fully individualized did not defend themselves. When attacked by the Mongols, the symbol of lower astral energies, the city suddenly sank into Lake Svetloja and at the same time it ascended to heaven. In other words, Kitesh was absorbed in a higher dimension of pure light. That is why it is also spoken of the ascension of Kitesh. Only the pure-hearted can still find the city and in calm weather they can hear the bells of the church of Kitesh.

In esoteric circles Kitesh is spoken of as the symbol of an unblemished cosmos. Kitesh is associated with the Grail (book 5), the symbol of a dynamic creative force that brings healing and renewal and opens in people the gates to higher states of consciousness, such as the imaginative consciousness. It is about the human being who awakens his inner spiritual core and often this happens in a quest, an initiation path.

In the Middle Ages, in what was then Russia, there was a brotherhood of knights who strove for honesty and inner nobility. They wanted to serve God, protect the homeland, and help the poor, the sick, and the infirm. These themes were also addressed in the West in the story of King Arthur and the Knights of the Round Table as well as the Percival legend (book 5). The human being who has purified his life path and is looking for inner chivalry can only find the grail if he leaves the integration human within himself and no longer thinks, feels and acts from a material, 3D consciousness.

Philosophy, astrology, alchemy, and Christian magic were practiced in royal courts and stately homes as in the rest of Europe. Russia was then under the influence of the highly developed Persian culture and the Kitesh legend played an important role there.

The Kitesh legend, like the Faust legend, is a major cultural legend, foreshadowing Russia's role in the future. Nikolai Rimsky Korsakov (1844 - 1908) turned it into an opera. The story runs like this. There is the high initiate Fewronia. She has endured superhuman trials and thus attained a higher form of consciousness. Then there are Little and Great Kitesh, built as fortresses of the primitive Christian faith, which at first was strongly esoteric. Inhabitants could follow their mystical path for seventy-five years and develop higher parts of beings in their souls. The monarch, Juri, had a deep mystical religious consciousness and served as an example to his people. Lady Fewronia, representing Lady Sofia, lived alone in a vast, wild forest in the company of birds, a bear, and deer. She knew about medicinal herbs and healed completely unconditionally and lovingly, her brothers, the people and the animals.

Then she meets Prince Yuri Vsevolod, the son of the king of Kitesh, who was lost during a hunt and roams in the wilderness badly wounded and weary. Fewronia sees the prince struggling with inner conflicts and wonders how a human can hunt his younger brothers to kill them. She notices that the prince has not yet discovered his inner light. He is still a believer who needs the religious institutions with their hollow rituals and imposed moral codes. He lives according to his educated mind and intuitive insight is totally foreign to him. It is up to Fewronia, who lives in perfect harmony with nature and her creatures, to assist the prince in the unfolding of his higher spiritual faculties, and in this she succeeds. She accepts his marriage proposal and goes with him to Little Kitesh. Fewronia is astonished to see the citizens of Little Kitesh at work, for they are nowhere spiritually standing. That fills her with pity. She tries to find an ear for her thoughts and to encourage the inhabitants to self-examination and personality development. But her goodness, love, light and strength appeal to few. The citizens of

Little Kitesh are focused on the matter and that has slowed down their thinking.

Meanwhile, the Tartars are advancing and approaching Little Kitesh. While Prince Vsevolod travels to Great Kitesh to warn them and ask for help, all the inhabitants of Little Kitesh are massacred except for Fewronia and a drunkard. The drunkard owes his life to showing the Tartars the way to Great Kitesh. Fewronia is taken as spoils of war and becomes the slave of the Kahn of the Tartars. The prince, who in the meantime has gone through inner spiritual purification processes and has become a pure grail knight, moves with his companions among the Tartars to free her without a fight and dies.

The citizens of Great Kitesh pray and ask the Heavenly Mother to envelop them with her pure powers and protect them. And the miracle is done, the city is shrouded in a golden fire-mist and becomes the head and heart of the world. The city sinks into the crystal clear Lake Swetlijar and at the same time it rises to the sky. This fills the Tartar army with terror and the warriors flee into the surrounding forests. Fewronia sees the ascension of Great Kitesh into another dimension and she travels with the city to the eternal light. There she is welcomed by the grail knights. Prince Vsevolod is one of them. Vsevolod and Fewronia become Grail King and Grail Queen of the resurrected Great Kitesh.

Source: pentagram.rozenkruis.nl;

Now we move on to Rudolf Steiner's "About Russia". The work is a collection of all the lectures where Steiner spoke about the Russians, their national spirit and their mission.

Today, in the fifth post-Atlantic civilization period, we live in the consciousness-soul-age, which began around the beginning of the fifteenth century. The result was the rise of the natural sciences and technology. The emerging bourgeoisie put the performing individual first and wanted participation in politics. Democracies developed slowly. Materialism entered into the picture. And so a ripe breeding ground for Ahrimanism appeared. All the more so since at the end of the 19th century, Ahriman and his followers were banished to Earth by Lord Michael. The result was the beginning of the industrial age.

In addition, we are preparing the sixth post-Atlantic cultural era. That is the Age of Aquarius or the Age of the Spirit Self, also called manas. According to Steiner, this era will start around the year 3,500. We also keep in mind that Ahriman will incorporate in a human form and he will physically walk the Earth around AD 3,000. This is only possible when material science has advanced so far that a certain physicality, with certain parts of the being, can be prepared. And that, of course, happens centuries in advance. Ahriman is already busy making ready the infrastructure for his physical arrival. A major part of this is the intensification of a materialistic medical science. The soul and the spirit must be abolished as living concepts, and medicines should only act on the material body. Then there is trans-humanism or post-humanism, which is currently being worked on with the famous DNA-modifying vaccines. The intention is to combine man and computer and to upgrade the human race to something that is no longer human, but Ahrimanic (cfr the Corona chronicles). Ahriman needs a body that is completely free from the affinity with Christ. It will probably be a beautiful and strong female body that will not age and may not die and he will probably incorporate in America. The Statue of Liberty is said to foreshadow Ahriman's coming to Earth in physical form

The incorporation will take place at a later age, as was the case with Lucifer in the year 3,000 BC and with Christ, around AD thirties. It will probably also happen during some kind of initiation. Once incorporated, Ahriman will do his very best to gain the largest possible following among the people. He will pose himself as the second reincarnation of Christ and he will deceive and tempt the people as much as possible. He will give them a clairvoyance and everyone will perceive different things. This will ultimately result in the struggle of all against all. Thus, Ahriman will seek to sabotage the Age of Aquarius and the evolution of mankind. It is up to the people to prepare and recognize Ahriman, thus escaping his Mephistophelic machinations.

In the Age of Aquarius, the center of world-defining events will be in the Slavic part of Europe. The spirit self, which is accompanied by an imaginary consciousness, will give people natural clairvoyance and we will be able to see into the etheric world (book 14). Humans will be able to enter the Shamballa and take in the ethereal Christ. A powerful Christ impulse will act on the people and give birth to a true brotherhood. That makes the Russian people, the Christ people par excellence. The Russian territory is the territory where people live who are directly associated with the Christ Impulse, people who in some way are constantly instilled with the Christ Impulse. The Christ constantly remains so present that he permeates the thinking and feeling of this people as an inner aura. Steiner then refers to the philosopher Solovjof as the preeminent representative of the Christ people.

But every step forward will be accompanied by opposing forces. Just as materialistic egoism is a major counter-force in our time, so egocentric subjectivity will be the great resistance in the coming age. Looking into the spirit world, many will imagine themselves a god. People will come to differing and contradictory points of view. The spiritual perceptions can become so subjective that people can attack each other fiercely and aggressively.

Steiner points out that the spirit-self-future is already foreshadowed in the Russian people. But the Russian coloring of the future only has a chance of success if fertilization already takes place now by the element of the consciousness-soul, from central Europe and more specifically Germany. The purpose of the Iron Curtain was to stop that conception. Moreover, secret societies are out to divert the Russian spiritual life from its destiny, so that during the spirit-self period, Anglo-American ascendancy is preserved. In book 15 we already talked about how Karl Marx was paid by the Illuminati to write his communist manifesto and how Trotsky was able to install materialist communism in Russia with the help of the CIA.

Steiner talks about the Russian national character who is talented and gifted, but without productive power. Russian souls have an absorbing capacity. It is Central Europe that must bring in the productive spirit in the East. It is the task of the fertilizing adjacent middle region to produce a vigorous spiritual life in its cultural development. And by this Steiner means not only idealism à la Kant and Hegel and other great German philosophers, but also anthroposophy. The Russian mind does not have that creative power, it is destined to receive rather than to form. You can see that by the way the Russian practices his faith. Byzantine religion has remained at the level at which it was received. Furthermore, the Russian man has an aversion to intellectualism and precise laws. He wants to be able to act on the hunches of the moment. He wants to be able to go his own way. He does not desire order and regularity or a centrally organized authority at all. Besides, the principle of the state with a tsar at the head, the Russians learned from the Tartars or Mongols, who conquered Russia and who had a Kahn at the head of their community. Another feature of the Russian national character is its peace-lovingness. His behavior is by no means expansive and imposing. Russians adapt and these characteristics make it easy for Russians to be abused and misled.

It is the mission of the Russian being to establish a connection with the Central European and Western European being, to absorb what the West produces and then to experience it and live it through inwardly. For the seeds for the development of the spirit self are rooted in Russian life. The Russian is essentially a dreamer, which makes him susceptible to Luciferic and Ahrimanian impulses as well. Ultimately, what was foisted on the Russian from the German territory, was Karl Marx's materialist communist manifesto and the introduction of Bolshevism by Trotsky and Lenin, who were the worst enemies of true spiritual development. And yes, the Russian absorbed materialistic communism eagerly and with religious fervor.

In Russia there is no close cooperation between the folk spirit and the individual human selves. There is actually still a kind of group spirit. The Archangel has not yet intervened in the national element. The national element still lives on in the Russian souls as a dream. The folk spirit has not yet been incorporated into the people. He connects with each individual Russian through the downward streaming light that radiates back, upwards from the earth, through the plants. That means that the Russians have a special relationship with their soil. Mysterious runes are present in what radiates from the inseminating with the sunlight of the Russian earth, and through those mysterious whispering runes the Russian folk soul speaks to the individual Russian. The popular spirit in the east of Europe works completely differently from the popular spirit in the West. The folk spirit of the Italians speaks through the sentient soul, that of the French speaks through the mind-soul, the English are addressed through the consciousness soul, the Germans through the I and the Russians through the spirit self that has not yet descended, and that happens via the reflecting light. So, it acts on the head, on the character of the mind, in such a way that images and feelings are formed, in preparation for the imaginative consciousness.

In the present era of the consciousness soul, antisocial impulses play a special role, for they must contribute to the individuation process. However, with the coming Age of Aquarius, the socialization phase is also approaching. The age of the spirit-self will bring people socially closer together. And this in such a way that a person really knows the other person, that he is interested in him as a person and that he really perceives him. Civilized people will then naturally stand against each other from their souls as brothers and sisters. But the spirit-self can only descend into a community of people permeated with brotherhood, and that community life exists in Russia, because they still have something group-soul-like there to cling to. Symbiosis must then be transformed into socialization. The blood brotherhood must evolve into a community of like-minded souls connected through spiritual science. In the Russian man a mystical nature will develop which is also intellectualistic and an intellectuality which is also mystical. Thus the Russian remains open to revelation, while well comprehending the descended truths from the transcendental world. In the West at the time of scholasticism with Thomas Aquinas, Albertus Magnus and Duns Scotus we had something similar here. There arose a collaboration between the thinking mind and revelation (book 6). In the next age, man will no longer need material proofs because then he can see into the spirit world. That presupposes that the Russian has to give up his institutionalized faith and his orthodox religion.

Marxist communism was actually totally alien to the Russian folk soul. According to Steiner, if a German engages in politics, he will fall into dreamy idealism that has nothing to do with reality. It becomes an untrue theorize, a pure illusion, an abstractly conceived representation, which is completely detached from any reality and which is yet implemented into real life. Such was the case in the former U.S.S.R. and we saw that in Hitler's Germany as well. Moreover, according to Trotsky, there must be a proletarian revolution for the whole world. If Schwab and his gang succeed in making their Built Back Better a reality and bringing agenda 2030 to the world, Trotsky's dream will be fulfilled. And I don't think that's must be the intention. Fortunately, Putin is not participating in this.

Goethe 's morphology

To write this chapter, while understanding and living through Goethe's life, work and thinking, I search the Internet and draw on Steiner's "Goethe's World View" and his "Goethe as the Father of the New Aesthetics". Here we go.

Johann Wolfgang von Goethe (1749-1832) was a famous German scientist, playwright, philosopher, poet, naturalist, amateur artist and statesman. He is what you call a "Universalgenie" in Germany. Versatile and complex, he deserves his place in this book as an original thinker. His attitude to life was "carpe diem" (seize the day). As a human being you have to get everything out of life. And the fullest life is one in which passionate fire and duty, as well as creativity and reasonableness, are in balance, because living with opposites invites classical perfection. Periods of deep despair alternate with periods of joy and intense happiness. Humans progress to maturity through mistakes, confusion, intelligence, ambition, friendship, and love. The tension between the need for unity, harmony and practicality on the one hand, and the desire for multiplicity, ambiguity, depth and wonder on the other, was central to Goethe's life. This tension could never be resolved and was the fundamental source of his creative energy. Transformation, personal growth and development towards autonomy and maturity is a core idea in Goethe's work. A certain philosophy is appropriate for every age of man. Children are realistic, they see what is there. The youngster who struggles with his inner passions becomes an idealist. But as a grown man, he has every reason to be skeptical. He doubts his methods and wonders if he will achieve his goal, but that keeps his mind moving as he learns from his mistakes. The old man becomes a mystic, who resigns himself to who he was, is and will be.

Goethe wrote several influential novels, including "Die Leiden des Jongen Werthers (1774) about a young man who commits suicide because of an unrequited love and also "Faust" (two parts 1808 & 1832). These works express a romantic rationalism. The first book was the culmination of the German Sturm und Drang period (1767 - 1782). It is about a group of romantic writers who glorify feeling, nature and the individual independent genius. Friedrich Schiller (1759 - 1805), a close friend of Goethe's, also belongs to this "genius period". Goethe and Schiller saw themselves as spiritual equals and coined the term "homo-geniality" for this. They inspired each other and wrote and published an awful lot. They are still seen as twin stars in the literary firmament. Together they studied things like the French Revolution, Kant's philosophy and aesthetics in art. In an extensive correspondence with Schiller, Goethe sought to define a theory of art, an aesthetic. Central to this science of the beautiful is harmony, self-realization and the transcendence of the True. Goethe loved ancient art and admired classicism. But he also found Greek art naive because there was no need to create a world that surpasses reality. The Greek mind was content with all that Nature generously granted. Nature was merely imitated there. And this realism did not satisfy Goethe, for the harmony in nature was the same as the harmony in the ancient arts. Goethe longed for more.

Goethe became especially famous for his "Faust". Professor Faust has been searching all his life for the ultimate knowledge to understand the world. One evening he studies a book of magic and manages to make contact with the Earth Spirit, but it rejects him. Finally, he makes a pact with the devil (Mephistopheles alias Ahriman). But the acquisition of Mephistophelic knowledge costs you your soul and therefore also your morality. Mephistopheles inspires the integration man, who starts from the materialistic world view and who only sees things through the glasses of his five senses. He is focused on the chemical world. The integration man sees the world and life as a machine and he ultimately wants to turn everything and everyone into machines. Goethe describes it like this:

> Who wants to understand a living thing
>
> First tries to drive out the spirit within
>
> Then he only holds parts in his hand
>
> But alas he lacks the spiritual link

As a politician, Goethe was employed by the Duke Karl August (1757-1828), where he took care of finance, road and mining, the army and the management of the court theatre.

The philosopher in Goethe studied Spinoza (Book 3) who at the time was hotly debated for being known as an atheist or pantheist. For Goethe and Spinoza, God equates with nature, and to love God means to love and know nature. He who knows nature knows God. For Goethe this was not a fantasy, but pure experience, phenomenology. Goethe did not believe in God, he beheld God. Because for him the only correct starting point for science and philosophy is the direct experience of natural objects. According to Kant, you could never know the thing 'in itself', but Goethe experienced that thing 'in itself' when he connected with nature. And although he considered Kant a great philosopher, dualistic idealism passed him by as if it were a fashion phenomenon. And in the end it was.

Certainly from the beginning of the 19th century, Goethe was convinced of the value of his own ideas. He regarded nature as a constant organic development in which polarity and intensification are an essential part of growth. Duality is for him the engine for progress. We also find this logic in Hegel (1770-1831). Hegel sees reality not as something static, but as the outcome of an evolution, in which new contradictions are constantly removed and a process arises in which something is becoming. He develops a dialectical system, which allows consciousness to examine itself. That's how it goes. You posit a proposition (the thesis), after which you deny it (the antithesis) and then arrive at a higher truth (the synthesis). Each stage of the dialectic contains all the previous stages, and each stage is given its own place in the Whole. Thus the individual, subjective Mind evolves through the objective Mind (the world mind in history) into the Absolute Mind (in art, religion and science). The Spirit comes to understand itself more and more in its expression as a collection of material, historical processes. It is therefore a process of becoming aware in which the Spirit strives throughout world history for complete self-development and absolute knowledge. In other words, history is the development of the consciousness of freedom because history is the development of the Spirit. Consciousness thus evolves into forms of consciousness that comprehend reality more and more fully, culminating in absolute knowledge (book 3).

This logic of Hegel is based on Goethe's conception of metamorphosis, with which he searches for the archetypal phenomenon, the original idea. But where Goethe ends, Hegel begins. Goethe proceeds in his philosophies of nature in such a way that from careful observation of phenomena he arrives at a thinking conception of the idea (primal phenomenon). Hegel wants to make the metamorphoses of the idea accessible to thought. He regards philosophy as the highest manifestation of the metamorphosing primordial idea of being. However, according to Steiner, neither Goethe nor Hegel really penetrated the spiritual world because they lacked self-perception and by this Steiner means thinking about your own thinking as he describes in his "Philosophy of freedom". There Steiner explains how thinking in concepts about reality becomes life in the reality of the spiritual world. Thus Steiner goes one step further than Hegel. Steiner perceives his thinking and thinks about his thinking. He talks about the living mind (books 6 & 14). Still, Steiner sees his anthroposophy as a continuation, broadening and deepening of Goethe's intentions.

Goethe's mind does not want to hold things to examine them. For him reason has to do with becoming, understanding what has become. Reason takes pleasure in development. Ultimately, he blames Hegel and Kant for creating a grand abstract system to explain a phenomenon that can be assumed in everyday life and in simple scientific observation, for Goethe possessed fine sensory and mental organs of perception that made it possible that nature could reveal the secrets of her being and her laws to him.

As a great philosopher, Goethe was not a creator of stand-alone systems of thought, a professional analyzer of arguments or a critic of contemporary cultural practices. The lectures on philosophy interested him only moderately. So, he wrote: "It seemed odd to me that I should tear up, isolate and, as it were, destroy those acts of the mind which I had carried out with the greatest of ease from childhood, in order to gain insight into the correct use of it. Of the business itself, of the world, and of God

I thought I knew about as much as the professor." Goethe's theory of being was rather organic. He felt one with living nature and he was a strong opponent of the Cartesian mechanistic worldview already in vogue at the time. Goethe did not recognize dead mindless matter and he did not wish to describe nature as isolated and secluded but as an active, living force, which penetrates the individual parts, from the whole. He imagines all of nature as "spiritualized". The Platonic splitting of the world into spirit and matter, as if it were two different worlds, seems very unnatural to Goethe. He regarded everything in the universe as working, as a manifestation of one and the same creative spirit.

As a scientist, Goethe researched, among other things, mineralogy, geology, anatomy (he discovered the intermediate jawbone in humans), physics and botany. He considered his scientific contributions as important as his literary achievements. He was extremely curious about science and intuitively he experienced the creative energy of nature like no other. He was therefore looking for the common archetype, the idea that underlies all animal species and ultimately humanity. This underlying idea, which can be seen in plants and animals, is inaccessible to the senses. They are the laws of development of life itself and they can only be seen with the spiritual eye.

Goethe became increasingly fascinated with botany and studied its pharmacological uses. He looked for a guide in Linnaeus (1707-1778), but gradually he became dissatisfied with his botanical system. Goethe thought it was an overly artificial, static and inanimate taxonomy of plants. Ultimately, Goethe's theory of morphology challenged Linnaeus' biology. Linnaeus focused only on the outward appearance of a plant. Goethe studied different plant forms in order to know the commonality that lives in them. He wanted to explain the multiplicity of the specific from the original unity. Rather, with his exact fantasy, he looked at the inner development and transformation that is characteristic of all living beings.

In 1778 he was given a garden by Duke Karl August. He also wandered around in the Thuringian Forest. While he scanned the plants with his material and spiritual eyes for growth and transformation processes. He traveled to Italy and examined the plants in the Alps and in the gardens of Padua. There he perceived the variable character of the plant shapes. Plants adapt to the environment in which they grow. Goethe carefully noted the processes that take place during germination and fertilization and growth, it became increasingly clear to him that the leaf is the basic organ of the plant and that the shapes of all other organs of the plant can best be understood when you regard them as transformed leaves. The leaf is the key to unlocking the secret, because plants get their shape from the interplay of their leaves. The basic organ of the plant is the leaf with the bud from which it develops.

A la limite, Goethe studied the life force (etheric body or form-force-body) in the plant and gradually discovered that all living organisms have an inner physiological "urge to form" (cf. Sheldrake's morphological fields in book 9). At the beginning of its development, the whole plant form rests in the seed grain. In this seed the primordial plant has assumed a form which, as it were, hides its ideal content in its outward appearance. The primordial plant then expresses itself in a succession of mani-festations, namely the stages from seed to stem to leaf, flower and stamen or pistil, as a kind of guideline through the laby-rinth of different forms of life. What Goethe did not perceive in reality, he could clearly envision in an imagination which he saw with his spiritual eyes.

The morphological method is thus a combination of careful empirical observation and a deeper intuition in the idea, the archetype, which directs the pattern of transformation over time as an organism interacts with its environment, because the same plant looks different as it grows in a valley or on a mountain, in a dry area or in the swamp, etc.

Morphology thus reveals the laws of transformation according to which nature produces one part through another and at-tains the most diverse forms through the modification of each organ. The idea or primordial phenomenon of a thing, in this case a plant, is thus an element that is directly present in it and acting creatively, in a purposeful manner. Because nature is intentional. The visible transformations are obvious, but the inner laws of nature, which make them necessary, are not. For Goethe, the world of ideas and the world of experience are not two separate, divided worlds as in Plato's world view (books 3 & 7). He perceives them at the same time. For Goethe there is only one source of knowledge and that is the world of experience in which the world of ideas is locked up. Goethe does not flee reality to build an abstract world of thoughts. He immerses himself in reality in its eternal change, becoming and moving, to find its immutable laws. He opposes the particular, the individual, in order to contemplate the archetype therein. Thus arose before his spiritual eye the primordial plant and the primordial animal, which are nothing but the idea of animal and plant.

If you think through this method of morphology further in your search for the primal animal, you end up with humans. For in the particular animal species one part is fully developed and clearly visible, while the other is only vaguely marked, and perhaps not at all perceivable to the eye. However, what is not visible in the animal is present in the original idea. In the primeval organism, all parts are fully developed and they keep each other in balance. The diversity of the individual arises because the formative power is completely focused on one part and another part, on the other hand, does not develop at all or only initially in the outward appearance. According to Goethe, a plant or animal species can change under certain circumstances into another species, because the force which produces a new individual in the process of reproduction is only a modification of that kind of force, which also effectuates the previous transformation of the organs in the course of growth.

In everything Goethe is looking for the idea which he can effortlessly contemplate, but which he wants to puzzle out. These ideas are not hollow schemes but driving forces behind the phenomena, and Goethe also seeks this idea in art. For him, art is the third realm next to that of the senses and that of reason, and the task of aesthetics is to understand this third realm. Goethe was very enthusiastic about the revival of classicism and traveled to Italy (1786-1788) to experience and study it up close. He felt very much at home in Italy. He found peace there and also devoted himself to science. He searched further for a model of the primordial plant, which makes it possible to fathom the essence of all plants, and there he discovered that the purposiveness of nature or of the creative spirit at work in it is also expressed in the great masterpieces, produced by creative people. He was confronted with Greek statues, that were made according to the laws of nature. He wanted to understand how nature brings about this process of becoming a work of art. Gradually he gains insight into the natural laws of artistic creation. Both in organic nature and in the work of art (painting, novel, poem, play) the creative yet opposing forces intensify into something aesthetic, which is at the same time unique and yet typical. By intensifying Goethe means the process by which the creative nature distillates the spiritual from the material. The operative in man is the idea. The process that also takes place in the totality of nature takes place in each peculiar human individuality: the creation of a reality from an idea. And man himself is the creator.

But for Goethe, the artist must go beyond Nature. He must go back to Nature with all the riches of a matured mind, with all that the new age has given to development. It is certainly not the task of the artist to imitate a reality, he must create an ideal reality. He must put the perfectly divine on this earth. For Goethe, the artist has a spiritual mission. His task is to grasp and develop the idea which underlies the thing but which in reality was prevented from unfolding itself freely. Artists must indeed work according to the eternal laws of Nature, but pure and free of all hindrances. Art should not start from what is, but from what could be, not from the real, but from the possible. The artist creates something from the sensory reality in the shape he himself gives it and thus he surpasses Nature, for his work of art is more perfect. Thus the Beautiful is a manifestation of Nature's secret laws, which would otherwise have remained hidden for eternity. The Beautiful is truer than Nature because it interprets what Nature would like, but cannot be. A real artist competes with reality and gives the illusion of a higher reality. The viewer of the work of art then feels a profound satisfaction, which is in no way inferior to a purely intellectual joy, because he is immersed in the heavenly inner peace and perfection of the world of ideas, for a work of art is ultimately a sensory appearance in the form of an idea. The Beautiful is no more and no less than the sensory real in a divine robe. The artist understands the art of raising the sensory reality in the divine sphere. The Beautiful is appearance that conjures up a reality for our senses, which represents an ideal world. The artist carries the world spirit further. Where Nature hands over creation, the artist continues it. Thus the artist fraternizes with the world spirit and art is a continuation of the process of Nature. Artists have a cosmic mission, because where the world spirit stops, the artist continues.

Goethe, as an excellent observer with his ordinary and extraordinary organs of perception, is also known for his color theory. He regarded this color theory as his life's work, but here too he encountered Ahrimanic materialism. While studying the great works of art by painters in Italy, he began to question how colors actually work. But no painter could tell him what was connection between color, light and shadow, or between the colors themselves. He consulted Newton (1642 -1727). But the then prevailing paradigm of Newton's optics did not satisfy his demand for knowledge.

For Newton, the white light that comes from the sun was present in all colors. Newton discovered that pure light, when refracted through a prism, breaks down into all seven colors of the rainbow, in the following order: red, orange, yellow, green, light blue, indigo, and violet. This pragmatically enabled Newton to quantify the angle bending of light rays and predict which colors would be produced at a particular frequency.

For Goethe, this conclusion was a mere hypothesis and the result of artificial laboratory research. There is no guarantee that in nature the light would react in the same way as in the experiment. Thus he began to observe the phenomena themselves, because for Goethe you have to start from the empirical observation of a great variety of particulars, in order to understand the primordial phenomenon which they all have in common. Its morphology is also based on this methodology. Only through careful observation of their interplay do we understand color, said Goethe, or as he defined it: "color is an elemental phenomenon in nature adapted to the sense of sight; a phenomenon which, like all others, manifests itself by separation and contrast, by mixing and association, by magnification and neutralization, by communication and dissolution: by these general terms its nature can best be understood.

Goethe concludes that color arises from the polarity of light and darkness. Darkness is not the complete impotent absence of light, as Newton and most contemporary theorists believe, but its essential polar opposite, and therefore an integral part of color. Darkness has an active power. It opposes and interacts with light and thus the colors are created. He then tested his theory against a number of experiments and in the process he discovered an oddity that seemed to refute the Newtonian system.

If Newton is right that color is the result of dividing pure light, then there should be only one possible order in the spectrum, according to the frequency of the divided light. But there are clearly two ways to produce a color spectrum: with a beam of light projected into a dark room, and with a shadow projected into a lit room. Something bright, seen through something cloudy, appears yellow. As the turbidity of the medium increases gradually, what appeared to be yellow, changes to yellowish red and finally bright red as its frequency decreases proportionally. Something dark, seen through something cloudy, appears blue; with decreasing turbidity it appears violet. The color produced also depends on the color of the material on which the light or shadow is cast. When a white light is projected above a dark boundary, the light extends a blue-violet fringe in the dark area. In contrast, a shadow projected above a light boundary produces a reddish-yellow border. When the distances between the projection and the surface are increased, the boundaries will eventually overlap. Done in a lit room, the result of the overlap is green. However, the same procedure performed in a darkroom produces magenta.

If Newton were right that only the bending of the light ray affects the given color, then neither the relative brightness of the room, the color of the background, nor the introduction of shadow could have changed the resulting color. Here too we see that, as in his morphology, Goethe takes context into account.

Moreover, Goethe's science is participative, for the observer's physiognomy plays an important role for him. According to him, there is a kind of inner light in the eye, because in the dark you can imagine all kinds of things. Goethe already had an imaginative consciousness (book 14) and in his worldview he recognized only two sources for all knowledge: the sense-perceptible and the ideal coherences of the sense-perceptible, which reveal themselves to the mind.

His thesis was that function underlies the developing organ. Nature forces the formation of the organs. If shape and color are present, it must be perceptible and recognizable. It must therefore be inherent in the nature of the eye that it also perceives the interactions which exist between the various perceptions. For the eye owes its origin to light. From arbitrary animal auxiliary organs the light calls forth an organ which must become its equal. And thus the eye is formed by the light and for the light, so that the inner light may meet the outer light. If darkness were the absolute nothing, then there would be no perception at all, when man looks in the dark.

Goethe's conclusion is that yellow is light dimmed by darkness and blue is darkness attenuated by light. That could explain why yellow creates a cheerful mood, because it is closest to light. Blue invites seriousness. It is closest to dark and feels cold. And so every color, in its interplay of light and dark, evokes a feeling. The reddish yellow arises by intensifying yellow towards the side of dark. This intensification increases his energy. The cheerful lively turns to ecstasy. As soon as this intensification goes even further from red-yellow to yellow-red, the cheerful, blissful feeling turns to turbulence. The violet is the blue striving for light. The cold and calmness of the blue turns into restlessness. This unrest is even greater in the blue-red. The stormy nature of the yellow diminishes, the peaceful calmness of the blue becomes more lively. The red gives the impression of ideal satisfaction, a reconciliation of opposites. A sense of satisfaction is also created by the green, which is a mixture of yellow and blue. But because in this the arousal of yellow is not intensified, and the tranquility of blue is not disturbed, by the reddish shade, the satisfaction will be purer than that which the red evokes. A sense of harmony and satisfaction is induced when we move its opposite next to a color. I am thinking of a garden with red roses in the midst of all kinds of greenery, or a room where yellow and violet set the tone, or a blue sky as the background of an orange flower tree. Anyone who dares to tan color in his interior or clothing shows character, he confesses colour and is therefor not a gray mouse.

And here we find again an example of an extremely original and sensitive thinker, who is not attached to matter and whom we also saw with great names such as Paracelsus and Hahnemann (book 15). But in the rising materialism, Goethe was soon not taken seriously as a scientist. His works were dismissed as amateurish efforts of an otherwise great poet. From the 19th century, Mephistopheles takes the helm even more firmly and the integration man continues to sell his soul.

After Goethe's death, his library came into the possession of Sophie van Oranje-Nassau (1824-1897), the Grand Duchess of Saxe-Weimar-Eisenbach. In 1896 she founded the Goethe-Schiller-Archiv, the oldest literature archive in Germany. At the request of the Duchess, Rudolf Steiner had also worked in that archive since 1889. The plan was to release a Goethe edition that would bring together the as yet unpublished works. Steiner's assignment was to edit some of Goethe's natural science writings for this edition. No one knows and understands Goethe better than Steiner and the Duchess knew that. Goethe is often referred to in Steiner's works and in Dornach we can visit the temple built by Steiner and named after Goethe, the Goetheanum.

Sources: Steiner's "Goethe's Worldview" & his "Goethe as Father of the New Aesthetics"; wikipedia; historiek.net, iep.utm.edu; britannica.com;

Sulfur Mercury Sal

At woudezel.nl, I bought seven works by Paracelsus which have been translated into Dutch. I will read, summarize and discuss a number of them for this book, so that we can also think along with this great mind. This chapter is about the three primal forces, sulfur, mercury and sal. In another chapter I will talk about the four elements and the pilars of the art of medicine.

In this work and in previous works I repeatedly point out the difference in thinking between the integration person and a person who individualizes. We are confronted with this difference in thinking every day, because it leads, among other things, to a split of humanity into sheeple on the one hand and wappies on the other. For the sheeple, a wappie is someone who adopts an absurd solution to a complex problem, preferably from other wappies. Wappies hang on outrageous (conspiracy) theories and are not open to facts and arguments. They mock reality as if it were fake news. Wappies are crazies who have lost their way. For the resistance, which mainly consists of so-called wappies, wappie is the nickname that the gullible sheeple, brainwashed and hypnotized by the politicians and the media, give to people - including highly educated such as doctors, scientists, lawyers, journalists, politicians, etc. - who use common sense and ask sober intelligent questions about corona policy.

Now it is remarkable that Paracelsus in his time already made a distinction between two ways of thinking. Thus for him there is thought which oversees the whole sphere of the spiritual life, and thought which is only focused on individual things. The one Paracelsus calls "the first thought," because it leads to the hidden spirit of things. The other way of thinking he calls a "public folly against the hidden wisdom." In other words, and we know that Paracelsus had a ready tongue, there is a human divine way of thinking and a beastly way of thinking. I think today we get to witness where this bestial way of thinking has taken us thus far.

In book 15 you can read about the Volumen Paramirum (1520), about what makes us sick and healthy. When Paracelsus wrote this he was 26 years old. There he was talking about the five entia. Steiner explains this entia as follows. The ens astral is about man as a being who is part of the whole great world, a man who is embedded in the macrocosm. The natural phenomena flow through him and sometimes have a bad influence on him. In addition, man is to a large extent an independent being. In the ens veneni he sees the physico-corporeal man as a whole that absorbs a certain cycle of substances and forces. He develops independently, gets to work with it independently. Paracelsus calls that integrated something de archeus, an inner master builder whom he also calls the alchemist. The inner alchemist separates the poison from the building blocks and it turns milk and bread into flesh and blood. For Steiner, the archeus is no more and no less than the etheric body or form-forces body. Now things can also go wrong here and then illness arises. Then there is the ens naturale, which separates man from the outside world. Man is the microcosm that reflects the macrocosm. Thus Paracelsus speaks of an inner heaven and an outer heaven, and he associates the inner organs with the planets. If the inner planets are disturbed, that is also a cause of disease. The ens spirituale deals with the effect of passions, soul movements, desires and drives, which, if excessive, have an effect on the physical organism. The ens dei tells how man is taken up into the divine world, as a creature of God and how the lack of spiritual development can give rise to diseases.

For Steiner the vehicles (parts of being) of man are:

* The material body

* The ether body

* The astrale body

* The spirit in which dwells the I

Paracelsus uses roughly the same terminology:

* There is the physical man, whom he calls the elemental man, composed of the same physical constituents, substances, and forces that we find everywhere in nature. In it

we find the archeus, the builder of the physical body. This physical body is twofold. On the one hand, there is the body that has grown from the semen of your father. That is the body of natural law. Congenital diseases find their cause here. On the other hand, there is the body that sustains you with what you eat every day. That is the body of mercy (the food that God provides and that we pray for). Bad eating and living habits can also lead to disease. But there is no disease for which there is no cure.

✳ The second man draws his powers from what lives in the stars. We are talking here about instincts, drives, desires, passions, lust and sorrow, sympathy and antipathy. This body Paracelsus also calls the astral body. According to Paracelsus, astrological astronomy provides more insight into this. When Paracelsus speaks of the stars, he is speaking of the astrality of man.

✳ The third part Paracelsus calls the Spirit, the divine spark in each of us.

Being ill mainly finds its origin in urges and passions (stars). Sickness is a result of an error of the soul, and in the end illness is the result of a lack of morality. Moreover, the stars in the firmament (above) have no influence on this in any way. Paracelsus also had a good laugh at the theory of temperaments and bodily fluids (book 15). For him this was a belief and certainly not something that came about through empirical observation and experience. Our manners and the qualities of our character are determined by the stars, while melancholy cannot be attributed to the stars.

Paracelsus further observes the Hermetic principle "as above, so below". Microcosm and macrocosm function according to the same laws. Man is made of the great world and he must live on what he is made of. The corresponding organ in the outer world is the remedy for the inner organ. In this sense, the right food and eating in moderation is the medicine par excellence. The human body absorbs, as it were, the body of the world. Heaven and earth, air and water are thus a man for science, and man is a world with heaven and earth, air and water.

When man is ill, the medicine must contain the whole firmament from the upper to the lower sphere.

Ten years after the writing of the Volumen Paramirum, Paracelsus treated the same subject (the cause of diseases) from a different angle in the Opus Paramirum. This book is intended for a wider readership. Here Paracelsus starts from three building blocks, from which everything is made. There are thus only three causes of disease and three corresponding drugs. It is about Sulfur, Mercuur and Sal as the primal forces of the world.

Let us first see what Steiner, who understood Paracelsus very well, says about this. Paracelsus looks far back to the origin of the earth, the beings that live on it and man. Millions of years ago everything had a different shape and everything was present in a rather fluid form. Man dwelt there in a rather spiritual state and he was much closer to the divine world. The whole animal world sees Paracelsus as humanity unfolded as a range. Paracelsus also saw that the human heart developed at the same time as gold was formed on earth. For him there is a connection between gold and the human heart. According to the ens naturale, there is also a connection between the heart and the sun. In book 5, I wrote a chapter on alchemy as a Christian continuation of the mystery-wisdom of antiquity. There I also discussed the underlying scheme. In this diagram you can see how in alchemy the inner and outer planets are associated with a particular metal, as well as the symbols that are used.

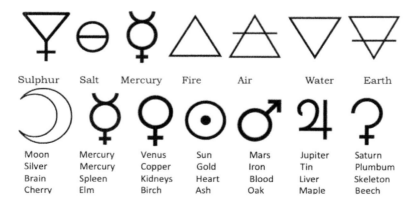

Sulphur	Salt	Mercury	Fire	Air	Water	Earth

Moon	Mercury	Venus	Sun	Mars	Jupiter	Saturn
Silver	Mercury	Copper	Gold	Iron	Tin	Plumbum
Brain	Spleen	Kidneys	Heart	Blood	Liver	Skeleton
Cherry	Elm	Birch	Ash	Oak	Maple	Beech

For Paracelsus, everything that arises as precipitation in the mineral kingdom is elemental and is represented by Sal. This also applies to the human physical body. Everything that remains as a liquid after certain precipitates have formed, is mercurial, changeable. For him also the soul is born of the same forces from which the mercurial, the mercury, is born. The origin of sulfur in the world parallels the origin and present form of the mind. We must be very aware that Paracelsus approached (sick) man from a holistic point of view, and that he examined the coherence of his vehicles. If a disturbance occurred there, he saw it as a disturbance of the magnetic equilibrium. Then he wandered with his intuitive gaze from the external sick organ to what lived in the inner soul of the sick person. And from there he went to the astral influences of the stars and to the elemental influences of the earth.

We now let go of "Steiner about Paracelsus" and examine for ourselves what Paracelsus communicates about Sulfur, Mercuur and Sal. Every material body, including that of man, consists of a combination of sulfur, mercury and sal. They are three substances in one form. So the physician must know these three substances and all their properties in the great world (macrocosm), then he recognizes them also in man (microcosm). Because there are as many diseases as there are qualities. Paracelsus also illustrates what these three substances are. When you set a piece of wood on fire, that which burns is sulfur. What goes up in smoke is mercury and what becomes ashes is sal. Every substance has its specific properties and they are always good. Disease occurs when a substance is missed. Then the other two increase and this creates an imbalance.

The effect of salt is purifying, expelling. It expels the poison from our organs, through the nose, ears, eyes and through other routes such as urination and defecation. Sulfur works by drying out and digesting the excess and Mercuur absorbs that which does not react to salt and sulfur. All diseases can be classified into three groups. Diseases from the salt cause a weakening, such as diarrhea, etc. The cure must therefore also be based on salts. All diseases that affect blood vessels, joints, bones, nerves, etc. arise from mercury. Syphilis in all its forms is a mercurial disease and must be cured with mercury. This can be metallic mercury and also ebony, juniper or antimony mercury, because mercury, like sal and sulfur, manifests itself in many ways. Mercury heals the tissues damaged by their own salt. Sulfur calms the internal organs.

As you can see Paracelsus was already working with the similarity principle and he condemned the classical (allopathic) doctors who fight cold with hot and hot with cold. For example, if you extinguish St. Anthony's fire by cooling, the fire will stop, but another ailment will appear. You have to fight disease with what the disease has produced. This healing principle, which is based on the principle of similarity, can be found two hundred years later in Samuel Hahnemann, the father of homeopathy (books 4 and 15). Hahnemann also warns that suppressing symptoms in an allopathic way produces different and sometimes worse symptoms.

In concrete terms, this means that you should never treat a burn with cold water, because then the heat will penetrate further into the body. You heal a burn with warmth, so that the heat is driven out of the body. So, for mercury diseases you administer mercury, for salt diseases, sal and for sulfur diseases, sulfur. The art of medicine then consists in correctly diagnosing the disease and administering the correct remedy. Meaning that you don't speak of jaundice, because everyJoe can do that, you speak of leseolus' disease, because leseolus cures jaundice. That also applies to eg Leprosy, here you speak of the disease of gold. And epilepsy is actually the disease of vitriol. But you still have to fine-tune it, for example, there is the viridellus epilepsy that is cured with viridellus. Paracelsus names the disease after the medicine. And again we think of Hahnemann, who invented drug diagnosis. He didn't care what illness he was dealing with. He just wanted to find the right cure. In homeopathy this is called repertorization. Where allopathic physicians first want to understand what they are dealing with, then do a lot of unpleasant to painful tests, and then label and treat the disease through painful, embarrassing and often degrading procedures, which are only aimed at eliminating the symptoms, for Hahnemann making the diagnosis and finding the right medicine go hand in hand. In se Paracelsus does the same. Both do not treat the disease, but the sick person with the individualized means, because every person is unique and special. The medicine is not selected according to individual symptoms, but according to the whole of the patient's physical and psychological symptoms, ie the clinical picture.

According to Paracelsus, illness can be the result of criminal damage, from the outside. Your time may also be running out. But often it is human nature that gives rise to the diseases. For example, sulfur develops an evil effect if an astral spark is thrown into it. I am thinking of a drive or a desire. Then the disease must be called by its name and cured with the appropriate means. There are many kinds of sulfur: resin, gum, turpentine, liniment, grease, butter, oil, brandy, etc. Some of them come from wood, some from animals, some from humans, some from metals such as gold, silver or iron oil, some of stones, such as the moisture of marble or alabaster, some of seeds, or other things, all of which are called by name.

The same goes for sal. Sal becomes rambunctious when dissolved by something astral. There are also many types of sal. Some are lime, others are ash, some are forms of arsenic, antimony, or marcasites, etc. These can all lead to separate diseases, which thus bear the particular name and properties of the respective sal. With dropsy you should give agents that dispel the dissolved salt. It's the same with mercury. It rises when the star of the sun sublimates it. The body is ignited by the constellation (astrality). The constellation causes the internal wars.

Man has his anatomy, his image, and diseases also have their anatomy. The doctor must study and know that. Then he has to find the remedy with the same anatomy. So every thing that is good for the female organism has its anatomy, and women's diseases are based on the same anatomy. Someone who has a disease with the anatomy of a rose should be happy that God also created the rose. And the same goes for the lily, lavender, etc. For every disease there is a remedy in the like, i.e., in that with the same (visible or invisible) image or signature. But nature provides the raw materials and the physician makes it into medicine. The rose must first rot and be born again in this death. Only then can you speak of medicinal powers. Paracelsus speaks of arcana, which are produced by art. From this spring the appropriate sulfur, mercury, and salt, in which lie all the secrets, the foundation, the work, and the cure. The medical artist has transmuted the raw material into medicine and the medicine in turn will transmute the body of the sick person into a new life. In Hahnemann's unitary homeopathy, the remedy is transmuted through dilution and dynamization (books 4 & 15). Paracelsus talks about separating and preparing. The medicine must be separated from the dirt it is in. The old nature of the medicine must first die and the remedy must be reduced to a new birth. This dying (rot) is the beginning of the division between good and evil. Thus the newly born medicine remains without any basic constitution, an empty arcanum.

So the three substances or primal forces grow into each other and are one. Each has its function to make the body complete. The body grows from sulfur. There are many types of sulfur. Blood is a kind of sulphur, flesh is a different kind of sulphur, the main organs another kind, the marrow another kind, etc. Salt gives strength to the body. Without sal nothing would be tangible. All processes of solidification have to do with salt. That is why there is always a different kind of sal present in bones, blood, flesh, brains, etc. Because just as there are different kinds of sulfur, there are also different kinds of sal. Mercury is the liquid. All fabrics have their moisture. Blood, flesh, bones, marrow, etc. each contain their own moisture. That's mercury. There is only one mercury with many different shapes and forms and the same goes for sulfur and sal. Now take a tree. If it loses its moisture, it dries up. If you take away its sulfur, it loses its shape, and if you take its sal, it loses its consistency. In the same way, diseases have a sulfuric body, a mercurial fluid, and they owe their stability to salt. Therefore, the drug must be digestible with regard to the three substances. It must be a consuming fire that takes away the disease.

It is important that the three primal forces know their rightful place in the whole. If one exalts (rises itself proudly) it is the beginning of disagreement. When sal elevates, cancer, ulcers, scabies, gangrene, etc. arises. The cause can lie in overeating, too much sense pleasure or the stars. When sulfur gets the high-hat, the body melts like snow in the sun. It is the four elements that transmute the sulfur, rendering it incapable of fulfilling its function and producing disease. Mercury rises due to heat added from outside. This can be heat from digestion (overeating), or heat from excessive exercise or heat from the stars. The whole body overheats and rages, as if it were in a high-pressure pot or still. The diseases of mercury can take various forms, such as insanity, rage, gout or sudden death. Fortunately, nature provides what is needed. Comfrey heals wounds eaten away by sal. What is dissolved by sulfur is restored by crocus and what has become too volatile by mercury is restored to its normal consistency by gold.

This is where the chapter on sulfur, mercury and sal ends. We now turn to Goethe's Faust. But first I wish to explain how Steiner associates Faust with Paracelsus. For it is no coincidence that this book has so far mainly been about Goethe and Paracelsus.

Steiner points out that Goethe and Paracelsus were, as it were, fused with their surrounding nature. Both are students of nature, both penetrate the objects of nature spiritually by observing and in both this leads to the great clairvoyant ideas about nature. It was all about the spirit in nature. Steiner suspects that the life of Paracelsus inspired Goethe in the portrayal of the figure "Faust". Neither Paracelsus nor Faust are satisfied with the various sciences. But Faust only merges in a certain way with nature after being separated from her. Where Paracelsus dies very early, Faust's path of development actually begins. In order for Faust to reach the same goal as Paracelsus, Goethe first makes Faust go through an inner, psychic path. Faust must first develop purely in the innermost part of his soul. He must awaken the spirit in his soul. Steiner puts it this way. Since Goethe had to raise his Faust from a Paracelsus figure of the sixteenth century to a Faust figure of the eighteenth century, he had to take into account that man no longer interacted with nature in such a direct and original way as Paracelsus. Faust thus became a character who can no longer discover the forces of existence, the meaning of being, by being directly fused with nature. He succeeds in this only through the hidden powers in the depths of his soul. Paracelsus was a child of his time, and Goethe had to make Faust also a child of his time, who learned to use reason and intellect from the natural sciences of his time, and who at the same time was also able to give form to it mystically. Thus Goethe expressed the whole revolution from the sixteenth to the eighteenth centuries in the development of European humanity. Paracelsus was then still able to obtain the deepest insights into nature from the development of soul forces through direct contact with nature. Two hundred years later, Faust first had to awaken the hidden powers of his soul, so that from the depths of the soul, higher sense powers may come to fruition. Thus modern man must not be fused with nature like Paracelsus, but by turning away from nature, experiencing the deeper soul forces. Only then can he come to a clairvoyant insight into nature.

Thus, the path from Paracelsus to Goethe is most interesting when you see how in the Faust figure comes to life from Goethe's soul what is essential for Paracelsus and also for Faust: that man cannot penetrate in the depths of the cosmos and the laws to which the eternal, immortal spirit of man is related, through the external senses, but only either through a direct association with nature, as in the case of Paracelsus, or through an unfolding of his higher senses, as in the Faust case. In other words he who want to approach nature without having developed the higher faculties of knowledge cannot understand the fundamentals of nature, nor recognize how the immortal spirit of man is related to nature.

Source: "From Paracelsus to Goethe" a lecture by Steiner in Berlin, 16/11/1911.

Faust

Let us now turn to the discussion of "Faust", Goethe's magnum opus and the greatest work ever in German literature. There are two books in front of me. "Faust", the dramatic poem by Johann Wolfgang Goethe, edited by Athenaeum, with the following text on the back cover. Faust consists of two parts. The first is a free stage adaptation of the medieval legend about a scholar who sells his soul to the devil for youth and success. In the second part, Goethe presents the vicissitudes of the man who strives for good through trial and error and who eventually becomes partaker of the eternal. Goethe wrote the entire work in rhymes and the book has been masterfully translated into Dutch in poetic form. And although Goethe called his piece a tragedy, it is full of humor and irony. The play, with its very refined instructions for its performance, far exceeded the possibilities of the stage at the time. It is therefore more intended for an imaginary performance. The entire stage score, with its overwhelming effects, humor, soap and poetry, invites the unbridled imagination of the reader to be activated. Goethe himself says that everything in Faust is written for "vision". Nevertheless, Steiner has succeeded in realizing Faust on stage. To this day, "Faust Weeks" are organized in the Goetheanum in Dornach, where the whole work is performed during a whole week.

The second book is Steiner's "Goethe 's Faust". On the back cover we read: the path of doctor Faust is the developmental path of modern man. Steiner's take on the Faust drama gives us insight into the secrets of us humans.

Let's first create a spiritual framework. In 1879, after forty years of struggle, the Michaelic hosts conquered the Ahriman armies. Ahriman and his companions were thrown to the earth and that ushered in the industrial age. Ahriman loves machines and technology and wants to turn people into robots. He inspires the short-sighted materialist thinker into the over-specialized scientist, the self-obsessed tech, the psychopathic banker, and the greedy economic man, so that they help him setting up his eighth sphere within this fourth. If he succeeds in doing so, and he is doing well, humanity development is over.

In book 14 you could read that Emil Bock wrote "The Age of Michael" and that in the chapter "The Confrontation with Evil" he tells that the anti-hierarchies in the spirit world were allowed to harass people on earth in every possible way, to bully them and to lure them into the abyss. For the gods want humans to endure any confrontation with Evil. Michael has thrown Ahriman down to earth, so that we humans can continue his fight here in the sublunar. In the Michael era it is the human who has to continue the battle with the dragon. The hallmark of our time, then, is that Evil appears openly. All the demons have been unleashed on the earth, and the gods trust that the humans will win the battle.

Ultimately, that is the theme of Goethe's "Faust". It concerns an impatient, unhappy, old professor who finds himself in the midst of a midlife crisis. He wants to decipher the riddles of the world, while his soul is not yet sufficiently developed to penetrate to the world of ideas, hidden in nature. Disenchanted, he mopes between his dusty books, which in no way give him wisdom. He detests himself and the empty nonsense he teaches his students. Faust, who longs for the absolute, as a spiritually melancholy person, suffers, so to speak, from depressive making materialism.

Meanwhile, a bet is made in heaven between Mephistopheles and the Lord, in which the devil is given free rein to use whatever means at his disposal to lead Faust astray. Mephistopheles thinks it will be a piece of cake. God, who thinks it to be a good idea to occasionally tease man with a harasser so that he remains awake and active, is convinced of the contrary. Mephisto who actually represents Ahriman also has Luciferic traits. Ahriman lies without a blink, while Lucifer presents you with illusions, playing pranks like Loki in the Edda. Goethe portrays him as a seasoned cynic who is at home in all worlds. He knows about homeopathy, military strategy, how to reclaim land from the sea by embankment and how to create money out of thin air, as the Khazar money changers à la Rothschild do to this day (book 15). He reduces human actions very simplistically to two motives, sex and money. For Steiner, Mephistopheles is the representative of what man has to overcome in the course of his deeper life experiences. An inner enemy of what man must pursue from the bottom of his being. Jung would speak of the archetypal shadow, which must be transformed and integrated during the individuation process.

Faust, who is actually fed up with the sciences, and feels dried up inside, says that he wants to experience life in all its facets. He turns away from world knowledge and he seeks self-knowledge. He wants to descend to the depths of his soul. He wants to get to know the macrocosm in the workings of his own microcosm. But he is not aware of this desire. Mefisto invades the old professor's life and promises him adventure and joie de vivre, but he is not clear on what he wants in return. The impatient, unhappy Faust, estranged from life, all too soon signs the contract with his blood, leaving him with the devil for life. Thus begins his personal path of initiation (book 14). Then Mefisto takes him along in the superficiality of party life and the highlights of sensual pleasure. He teaches Faust how to escape depression through sex, drugs and rock and roll. And that while Faust, unconsciously at least, is looking for depth and authenticity. He has completed the integration-man in him and he wants to individuate.

Together they literally fly out the door, while Mefisto turns his jacket into a hot air balloon. They arrive at Auerbach's cellar in Leipzig, a café filled with tipsy, babbling and singing drunks. Mefisto offers wine, quarrels with the drinkers and scares them with illusions and sorcery. When the whole thing goes crazy and is upside down, he and Faust quickly get away with it.

Then they end up in the witch's kitchen, where the witch, at the behest of Mephisto, gives Faust a lust-inducing potion and turns him into an attractive young man. In the mirror Faust already saw a beautiful maiden with whom he falls in love. It is as if Faust now turns to drugs under the influence of a bad friend and seeks his liking in illusions. Mefisto works as the best behavioral therapist, who wants to help Faust to overcome his depression by encouraging him to go outside, make friends and find a lover. So he encourages him to deal allopathically with the inner pain and emotional death by suppressing the painful psychological symptom. In the meantime, we know that new and worse symptoms will then appear.

The next scene takes place on the street, where Faust, as a horn-dog, is harassing a young girl of fourteen. It's Gretchen. But the child does not want to know about it at first. With the help of Mephisto's wiles, Faust can turn Gretchen's head and swoop in on her. Gretchen loses her brother in a duel with Mefisto. Her intuition warns her of the devil, for in his presence she feels fear and disgust. But Faust talks that out of her head, he does not take her high sensitivity seriously and does not listen. Like a purebred pedophile, he manipulates the naive, good-natured teenage girl, who falls deeply in love with him, and makes her pregnant. Long story short, the maddened Gretchen, afraid of being cast out, drowns her baby in utter despair, kills her mother and ends up in a dungeon.

All this passes by the completely unconscious, ignorant and selfish Faust, while he celebrates a pagan feast on Walpurgis night with Mephisto and a number of witches. There is dancing and singing and drinking. But when he wakes up from his intoxication, he discovers what happened to Gretchen. He is rushed off his feet and with the help of Mephisto he wants to free her, but the girl repents and wants to atone for her sins. She breaks away from Faust and dies. Her soul has been saved and Faust remains helplessly devastated with a terrible hangover.

Then the second part begins. Faust is sleeping in a field and at the request of the angels he is healed of his trauma by the elves. The next scene takes place in the Imperial Palace where Mefisto is applying for the role of court jester. The empire is in bad shape. The country is in moral decay, there is robbing and looting everywhere. The rule of law is completely gone. And the treasury is empty. Poverty everywhere. Mephisto tells the emperor that there is enough money in the ground where all those gold pots are buried. You just have to bring them up, he says. But the concerns are quickly dismissed as irrelevant, and the court celebrates for many pages, with much tumult and much singing, an Italian-style carnival. A procession of masked courtiers with all kinds of characters and allegories passes by. The living tableaus parading past range from playfully erotic to vulgar obscene. Then a chariot floats in on which Mephisto is depicted as the miser and Faust as the god Plutus, who conjures pure gold from a seething incandescent cauldron. .

And money is indeed conjured up out of thin air when all imperial debts are cleared with paper money backed by the (nonexistent) buried money pots. Mephisto teaches the emperor how to create money out of thin air and to pay with fiat money. The denominations are distributed among the creditors and everyone is satisfied. The city is buzzing with pleasure again, while paper money circulates profusely. The emperor is rich again. But he is not satisfied, for now he wants to see Paris and Helen of Troy in person. So Mefisto's sorcerers' pranks are again invoked.

But Mephisto doesn't like that. For this they must go to the realm of the Mothers, the watchmen over all forms of the past and present. In other words, the Mother Kingdom is the area where the eternal archetypes of all that exist are preserved. Mephisto doesn't belong there. The material world is his element. After all, hell is nothing but condensed matter. A Faustian man passes through the material to enter the eternal, divine, for that is also where his origin lies. A Mephistophelic man cannot detach himself from the material. The first goes for wisdom, the second for scholarship. Faust receives the key to the spirit realm from Mephisto and Mephisto stays at home. Faust has to get a tripod. With the tripod he can evoke the image of Helena and Paris. While Faust is on his way to the realm of ideas and back, Mefisto kills time selling beauty ointments to chicks.

Then everyone goes to the knight's hall to watch the shadow play. Our fantasy is invited to see a scene in the stage and Mefisto presents himself as a prompter. Faust uses the tripod to project the images of Paris and Helena to the frequent comments of the public. But Faust loses the distinction between reality and appearances and falls instantly in love with the beautiful Helena. The piece is called "the robbery of Helena", Faust does not agree and wants to save Helena. In the commotion the tripod explodes and Faust falls unconscious to the ground. Mefisto loads him on his shoulders and takes him away. According to Steiner, Faust is ripe to penetrate the spiritual world. He can spiritually elevate himself to the eternal archetypes. But he wants too impetuously to get hold of the divine goal. He is still too much tied to the material and he must first go through all the material phases in order to reach the final goal, completely purified. That is the initiation path of life itself.

Faust wakes up in his old study on the bed. The room is affected by time, dust and cobwebs. In the next chamber is a laboratory. There, his former assistant, Wagner, as if straight out of Huxley's "Brave New World", creates a human being in a goblet, a homunculus. Wagner symbolizes the scholar who gets stuck in the field of abstract scientificity, he is attached to the sensory world. He is the integration-man par excellence.

Homunculus can move freely through time and space in his bottle and he can also move in a person's mind. He sees the interior of the sleeping Faust. Homunculus is actually a spirit without substance, who wants to act and for that he needs a body. His tremendous urge for reality takes Mefisto, Faust and himself to Greece in search of Helena. They land there on Walpurgis Night and spread between the Beltane fires. They interrogate sphinxes and sirens and nymphs. Many figures from Greek mythology, as well as classical philosophers, are presented. You could say that Faust and Mefisto are now immersed in the Jungian realm of archetypes. Griffins, centaurs, magnified ants, dwarves, sirens and sea dwellers inhabit a surreal landscape. In any case, Goethe shows an enormous knowledge of Greek mythology here and the archetypes are flying around your head. Steiner also talks about the human being who descends into the soul world, so that ever higher secrets are revealed to him in ever deeper regions of consciousness. Then the world of sensory experience and the mind takes on a new meaning. It becomes the "likeness" of the eternal. Man realizes that he must close the bond between the outside world and his own soul. Then the unattainable is reached and the riddles of the world are solved.

Chiron takes Faust to Hades, where he hopes to find Helena. Mephisto ends up with the Fates who disguise him as Helena's ancient palace guard, and Homunculus leaves with Thales and Anaxagoras for the Aegean Sea to be truly born. He has to start at the bottom of the food chain and go through all the stages. Eventually he no longer exists as a ghost and mixes with the elements. The spirit has to pass through matter to become a perfect human being.

The next scene takes place in front of the palace of Menelaus in Sparta. There on the beach is Helena. She has just returned from Troy conquered by the Greeks and wonders what role she will play. Wife? Queen? POW? atoning sacrifice? She must go from Menelaus to the palace, inspect everything and then prepare everything for the sacrifice. She does this with the help of the old palace guard, Forkyas, alias Mefisto. But there is no sacrificial animal. Who or what will be sacrificed to the Olympian gods? Mephisto says that she herself will be slaughtered. But there is a way out: a marriage to Faust. Mephisto takes her as if by magic to the Faust palace. Faust, dressed in a medieval knightly court dress, descends the stairs with dignity. He kneels before her and gives her all his possessions. But Helena speaks a different language. That is expressed in another verse form. Like Sofocles, Helena speaks in rhymeless, metrical verses. Faust teaches Helena to speak his language by teaching her to rhyme. This play of rhymes seals their union and from it comes a son, Euforion. But great songs don't last for ever. Euforion wants to be free and to fly like Icarus, he jumps from a high rock and crashes down to the ground at the feet of his parents. His physicality dissolves and rises like a comet to the sky. His robe remains. Helena then dies in Faust's arms, her physicality disappears, and her robe and veil remain in his arms. Then Helen's robe and veil dissolve in the clouds, which envelop Faust and lift him up.

Steiner sees it this way. Faust's love for Gretchen in the first part was a sensuous love. His love for Helena in the second part is rather an image for the deepest mystical soul experience. Faust seeks the eternally feminine in the depths of his own soul. Helena, as the Greek archetype of the most beautiful woman, represents the woman in man, the Jungian anima. The connection with the eternal feminine gives rise to the child in man, which is imperishable and belongs to the eternal. The lower life must die before the higher can be born. The second part of Goethe's Faust pictures an initiation, the birth of the higher man from the depths of the soul. Goethe knew this all too well when he said, "Let the general public rejoice in what is outwardly displayed, to the initiate the deeper meaning will be apparent."

According to Steiner, the marriage between Faust and Helena cannot be permanent. Descending into the depths of the soul is possible only in exceptional moments of life. You then dive into the regions where the spiritual is born in its highest form, but after this profound transformation you return to the active life. The euphoria is over and you have to move on, while you are married for good to eternity. Faust has married his feminine soul. An alchemical wedding, à la Christian Rosycross (book 6). This makes him become absorbed in the all. From now on Faust will lead a double life, a life as a mystic and a creative life in matter. For Carl Gustav Jung, "Faust" is indeed an alchemical work. Reading it pierces through the top layers of your unconscious and sinks into the depths of your psyche, much later it comes back to the surface in another form, where it testifies to a long-lasting effect. Jung is talking about the process of individuation, in which the unconscious with its personal and collective archetypes, such as the anima and the animus, are integrated into the conscious (I) into the greater, all-encompassing self. Steiner speaks of man who seeks within himself the divine voice that calls him to the marriage between the eternal masculine, the world and the eternal feminine, consciousness. The eternal feminine takes us upwards. In other words, Goethe attempts to build a bridge between self-knowledge and world knowledge through natural knowledge. Faust's outward life will henceforth be the life of a man who has given up his existence in order to exist. From this out he will work entirely selflessly in the service of mankind.

In the next scene, the cloud hits a high mountain peak, descends on a plateau, splits and Faust emerges. He awakens from a blissful dream where he briefly lost himself in Gretchen's effigy. Then there is Mefisto and Faust tells him that he dreams of a project. He wants to perform deeds. He wants to win land from the sea and Mefisto has to help him with that. But first they have to fry a bigger fish. The Emperor, who only wanted to amuse himself, is in distress. His country is in ruin and everywhere the battle is raging. The people who want peace chose a new (counter) emperor.

Emperor and Counter-Emperor now face each other with their armies in battle array and Faust's plan is to help the real Emperor conquer and then get the beaches on loan, as a reward. This succeeds thanks to the illusions of Mephisto, who, as it were, hypnotizes the opposing army. The enemy is fleeing in terror. As a reward, the emperor distributes land and property to the feudal lords who fought at his side. Whoever joined the counter-emperor loses land and property. The church claims a great deal of the treasures because the victory has been won by devilish wiles and deceit. The emperor has to buy off his heaven and has hardly anything left.

The next scene takes place on the diked area. Entire meadows, fields, forests and villages have been reclaimed from the sea. The water works have taken their toll, people have been injured and died. Nevertheless, the result is a beautiful cultural center. An old couple, Baucis and Philemon, live in a house on a dune. They rescued and cared for the drowning. Faust is now very old. He lives in wealth in his palace. But the hut on the dune of the old couple is a thorn in his eye. They ring the bells of their chapel too often and that makes Faust mad. He has offered them a nice house elsewhere, but Philemon and his wife decided to stay. Meanwhile, Mefisto, who is a privateer scouring the seas, comes home with a rich booty. Seeing Faust's frustration with the two old folks, he sets their house on fire. Baucis and Philemon die. That night four gray women come to visit. They are called Lack, Gross Debt, Distress and Worry-burden. Worry-burden slips into the palace, the other three make a run for it, for they no longer have a hold on Faust's life. Faust has finished them, so to speak, transformed them.

After a discussion with Faust, where Worry-burden appeals to his conscience and asks if he can really stand with his life balance in the face of eternity, she blows in his eyes and hits him with blindness, because Faust in his life was not freed from magic. His actions did not come from his own strength and he knows it. His blindness brings him one step closer to death, but that doesn't stop him from starting his next project, draining a poisonous swamp. Behind his back, however, the ghostly lemurs are digging his grave. Then the very elderly Faust dies of natural causes. Mephisto wants to take his soul. But he can't. Faust has lived with the best and deepest of his being in eternity since his Helena period. This eternal takes full possession of him after his death. The angels expel Mephisto with love and rose petals, and they carry Faust's soul to heaven. Mephisto is left disappointed and heavily acting all wounded.

The medical art of Paracelsus

We descend back to the sixteenth century and the medicine of Paracelsus, where we start with the book Paragranum. In this work Paracelsus explains the foundations of true medicine. The book is one big tirade against mainstream medicine, which is based on the theories of Celsus, Galen, Avicenna and Aristotle, and who see illness as an imbalance between the four body fluids, namely: blood, mucus, yellow bile and black bile, which in turn are associated with the four temperaments, namely: choleric, phlegmatic, sanguine, and melancholic. For Paracelsus, this has everything to do with fantasy and belief. That's the bullshit they teach in the universities and it's pure deception. As a result, patients are mutilated, destroyed and killed by these self-absorbed impostors, for they all try out anything while they hope for the best, while making big money. The healing art of Paracelsus is based on knowledge and experience. He knows exactly what he is doing, why and with what consequences.

Paracelsus also opposes Vesalius, who based his anatomy on the dissection of dead people and animals and on the vivisection of living animals, without any anesthetic. For Paracelsus, anatomy means the formative forces, the invisible creative principle that reveals itself in all phenomena, each time in a specific recognizable way. Every disease and every associated medicine has its own specific anatomy. Hahnemann, the father of homeopathy, spoke in this case of the disease picture and the corresponding drug picture (books 4 & 15). Both, Paracelsus and Hahnemann, proceeded from the principle of similarity.

In the Paragranum Paracelsus sets out his worldview. The Hermetic expression "as above, so below" sums it up. The cosmos is the great man and man is the small cosmos. To get to know and understand man and his diseases, you have to know how the macrocosm works. The macrocosm existed before man. The doctor must therefore know what was before man. Paracelsus divides the macrocosm into two parts. On the one hand, there are the upper elements, air and fire (the constellation), which are the field of research of the astronomer or astrologer. The bottom two elements are earth and water. That is the field of research of the philosopher. By philosophy, Paracelsus did not mean moral philosophy or ethics or any other nonsense à la Erasmus. His philosophy provides insight into the functioning of the material body. With astrology Paracelsus aims at the invisible forces and workings of the astral and not the starry sky. Philosophy and astrology, alias the knowledge of the four elements (earth, water, air and fire) are the first two foundations of paracelsic medicine. The other two are alchemy or spagyric and ethics. By alchemy Paracelsus means the art of producing arcana by means of separation. Those are disembodied, spirit-like drugs. In other words, alchemy includes all preparations, properties and arts with regard to the four elements mentioned. This art of creating recipes is based on anatomy, in such a way that organ with organ, arcanum with arcanum and disease with the corresponding disease, is associated. Ethics is about the character of the physician.

First let's talk about the first two foundations, which we find in the macrocosm. This is explained in great detail in his book "The four elements, the mothers of the world". It is not so much a medical tract as a cosmogony worked out in detail. Paracelsus speaks of the four primordial substances, earth, water, air, and fire as the producers of fruits. They secrete something, as it were, or they exhale something. An element is something that produces things. It's a mother. The elements themselves are an empty form, made of invisible matter, just as the mind of man is invisible. And these elements in turn, like everything else in the world, consist of a composition of sulfur, mercury and sal. These three do not derive their character from the element, the element derives its own from them.

The four elements originated from paradise and paradise has been moved to another place. The four elements arise from the yliaster. Paracelsus then speaks of the four yliasters. When the world year is over, everything will be swallowed up by the yliaster again. After this, another world will follow, one which, like the soul, will not perish, but will endure. Presumably Paracelsus means here the fifth sphere, where the element earth (matter) will have disappeared and where we humans will have ascended as the tenth hierarchy to the level of the present angels.

The material body as a part of being (vehicle) will no longer exist, while we will have developed higher parts of being.

For Paracelsus, the earth is material, sticky and clinging. Water is wet. The fire is the firmament (the stars) and it can be hot and cold. The air is the heaven that encloses everything and is both hot and cold and both dry and humid. The four elements are made up of two groups, air and fire on the one hand and earth and water on the other. The air carries the fire and the earth carries the water. Air and fire carry earth and water. They are made so that each time one wears, uses and nourishes the other. Thus space consists of two spheres, an inner and an outer, each containing two elements.

First, God pulled the sky out of the yliaster. Then He set apart the fire, and so forth. Thereafter God has organized the elements. Out of the sky came chaos, the seat, the chain and the soil; from the fire day and night, Sun and Moon; from the earth the trees and herbs, grass and fruit, from the water ores and stones. In this structuring process, something else is always born from what remained.

The cosmogony of Paracelsus is geocentric. The earth hangs still in the sky, like the egg yolk in its egg white, and the sun and the stars revolve around it. In winter the sun does not give heat because it lies fallow. The Moon is the phoenix of the firmament, dying and being born again. The same thing happens with the other stars.

So the Master Builder first separated the air and then organized the air. Air's job is to serve as a home for the three other elements. Air encloses all that is perishable, and separates it from the eternal. She holds the world together. It is also the breath to which all things owe their life. Everything needs air, man, the earth, water and fire. Thanks to the air, the fire (firmament) lingers. It is an invisible chain that holds up and carries the firmament. This happens because of its chaos, that is the space between heaven and earth, the space where people and animals live and plants grow. You can see the earth as the yolk of an egg. The white is the chaos, which keeps the earth in place. The sky also carries the firmament. The stars float in the air and continue their orbits there, like the birds flying in the sky.

The Master Builder then organized the fire. From the air the heavens arose, from the fire, the firmament. The fire, those are the stars. In the fire there is hot and cold, light and darkness, and also burning and freezing. The material fire we use Paracelsus calls "tristo" and we find that in the four elements. In the water it is expressed in steel and stones, in the soil it is expressed in the fruits and so it is in the air.

The firmament was organized as follows. First the white glow was taken out. Mass and matter were made of it. That's the Sun. The red translucency that remained is in the Moon and the stars. The heat and the dryness are in the white light of the Sun. The red glow is cold and damp and belongs to the stars and the Moon. The element of fire, therefore, can be found in the sun and the stars and what they produce towards the earth, such as snow and rain, wind and hail, cold and warm, day and night, summer and winter. For there are stars of the wind, stars that breathe out the dew and mist, stars that cause thunder, and stars that pour out the clouds. The snow stars blow snow and fine hail. Furthermore, there are thunder and lightning stars and stars that make rainbows.

There are also seven kinds of planets that make seven kinds of metals. They are different from the terrestrial metals produced by the water. Then there are the stars that cast out gem stones, garnets and other rock shapes. Some stars make rubies, others sapphires and still others emeralds. These stones are born from the stars that are next to the planets. They are thrown to the earth and you will find them in the upper layers of the earth. Crystals and beryls come from the snow stars.

The next book is about the element earth, which produces all food. The earth was materialized into a sphere placed at the center of the world and containing all the powers of the plants, trees, herbs, and crops that grow on it. In this book Paracelsus goes very deeply into the characteristics, tastes, compositions (from sulfur, mercury and sal) and functions of the plants, trees and all kinds of crops. Then he talks about the element of water, which comes out of the depths of the earth like a tree with trunk and branches, which run over the earth like streams, rivers, creeks, water courses and which flow into the crown, the oceans. The water also has its fruits. Those are salts; minerals, including metals; gems and stones. All these products of the element water are again extended and discussed in detail, for all these products of the earth and water are the raw materials given by nature, from which the alchemist extracts his medicines.

We now return to the Paragranum. It states that the doctor must look for man in the four elements. Not four people, but one man in the four elements. And in the four elements he must learn what is wrong with this man. The physician must learn to apply the outward man (macrocosm) to the inward and to recognize the inward in the outward. God created the outward man so that we may come to know man through it. When we have insight into this, we can then apply what we have learned to the individual man. The physician must carry within himself a complete picture of the anatomy of the outward man. Anatomy should be compared to anatomy and organ to organ. Finally, the physician will understand that arsenic is cured by arsenic, realgar by realgar, the heart by the heart, the lung by the lung, and the spleen by the spleen. But not through the spleens of cows! No pig brains for man, but the brain that is the outer brain of the inner man. The organ of the great man out there heals the organ of the inner man. For the microcosm and the macrocosm are formed of the same four elements. The thing is, you have metals in the water, the earth, the air, and the fire. Similarly, there are four kinds of lemon balm, four kinds of Mercury, four kinds of amethyst, four kinds of snow, and so on. The doctor needs to know all that. Man is fourfold and so is the medicine.

The physician must further recognize the celestial bodies in the body of the microcosm. For the stars in the body have their properties, nature, essence, kind, orbit, position and proportion, just like the stars in the outside world. They differ only in form or substance. Their powers are the same. You must know that the constellation in heaven has no physical body, and it is the same in man. Likewise, the disease is not material. In man are the Sun, the Moon and all the planets, and so in him are all the stars and all the chaos. The inner heaven thus works in us. The doctor must be able to translate the macrocosm to the body. All planets in man have their likeness, their signature and their children and the (outer) heaven is their father. Heaven and earth, air and fire is the father of man. And man is related to his father. As the father is, so is the son, with a liver, spleen, brain, and so on. For the doctor, the father reveals the son. Thus heaven and earth, water and air, reveal man. The anatomy of man is based on the anatomy of the macrocosm (his father). Because man is part of the earth, he must eat of the earth. Because he is part of the water he must drink of the water, because he is of air he must breathe and he needs heat because he is of fire.

When the inner ascendants, signs, planets, and the like rule in the course of the microcosm and are eager for the outer firmament, they attract it as the earth attracts rain. If what man attracts from heaven is healthy, then it is good. If not, it's poison. Sickness and health thus arise from heaven. The heaven-caused diseases can be divided into two groups. One is, the other is not subject to medicine. Subject to medicine are only those diseases which heaven produces by its poison. Not subject to medicine are the diseases over which heaven has power and which it will not relinquish. They cannot be treated by medicine. The real doctor knows the difference.

There are as many disease states as there are stars. The names of the diseases are the names of the stars. There is the disease of Mars, that of Luna, that of the Sagittarius, that of the Leo, that of the North Star, that of the Bear. The same applies to health. Anyone who knows the origin, essence and nature of the rain, therefore also knows the origin of the diarrhea in its various forms. He also knows what is needed and what their properties are. Anyone who knows the origin of the thunder, the winds and the storm, knows where colic and stomach cramps come from. Who knows how hail and lightning arise and grow, what is in them and what it is, knows the urine, the stone and the grit and everything of the tartarus that has to do with it. Whoever is able to see the conjunctions in context and knows the darkness, knows the sudden death, the stroke and all that goes with it. Anyone who knows the new era and how cracks appear in it from day to day, from hour to hour, knows about fevers. Who knows what the rust of the planets is and what their fire, their salt and their mercury are, knows how proliferations grow and where they come from, as well as scabies and leprosy and gnawing sores. Who knows what Venus is guided by and what it contains, knows the troubles of women, their diseases and health; and so it is with everything.

The physician knows the invisible, which is not material and yet has its effect. The diseases are from heaven, heaven rules the diseases and the diseases are invisible. Sicknesses are not material forms, therefore spirit must be used against spirit. The medicine is invisible, the effect is visible. What we see is not the medicine, but the material form in which it lies. The arcana of the elements are invisible, and so are those of man.

Regular doctors think the other way around. They look for the disease in the bodily fluids and claim that the diseases originate there, while the bodily fluids are produced and made by the disease. Paracelsus makes the following comparison. The snow does not make winter, it is winter that makes snow and it is not by cleaning up the snow that you dispel the winter. Even if there is no snow in the whole country, it is still winter. This is also how you should look at the diseases, because they arise from the stars.

The anatomy of the body and of its properties has its foundation in the outside world. For as it is outside, so is it in man, and what is not outside, is not in man. The outside and the inside are one and the same. It is one constellation, one influence, one correspondence, one time, one ore, one tereniabin, one fruit. Adam's limbus was heaven and earth, water and air; therefore man remains in the limbus and he contains and he is heaven and earth, water and air. That means that you cannot be a doctor without philosophy and astronomy.

The astronomer applies the stars in the lower sphere and the philosopher the minerals in the upper sphere. So mineral and star are the same. Thus, Mars is iron and iron is Mars. It is one and the same anatomy that appears in all four elements. Thus there is a Saturn in heaven which is of fire and there is one in the earth which is terrestrial. Thus there is a Sun in the sky and there is also a Sun in the water. And so there is everything in quadruplicate.

The true physician is the inward astronomer and the inward philosopher, born of outward astronomy and philosophy. The physician should not look directly at man, but at nature and all that is contained in heaven, for that is what man is made of. Man is an image in a mirror set in by the four elements, and when the elements perish, man perishes too. You can therefore only know a person through insight into the outside world, of which he is the mirror image. There is no part of man's body that does not encompass the vault of heaven and it is displayed in hundreds of ways. The substance, the appearance and the essence are the things the doctor has to deal with. You have to build up the whole man from the things in the outer world, then you will find in him the graphic forms of all materials, and in them all the appearances of the organs, healthy and sick; moreover all their essences, what one has to do with the other, what damages and what makes whole. The upper and inner constellations are one and the same, they have the same powers. The outer heaven is the signpost of the inner heaven. The true physician understands that the same anatomy can be recognized in the small world as with the relevant plant in the large world. This doctor therefore speaks of Melissa's disease or Savina's disease. In other words things similar to each other must also be associated with a similar name, for the works are based on this comparison, i.e., by this, the arcana against the resp. diseases are revealed. For there is not only one kind of colic, but many kinds, as many as there are arcana against colic.

So philosophy includes all organs and all body parts, health and disease. Thus the judgment of urine must be learned from the outside world, the pulse is felt in the firmament, the physiognomy recognized in the constellation, the chiromancy in the minerals, the breath in the wind from east and west, the fevers in the earthquakes, and so each time one has to do with the other. If the physician masters from word to word the things in the outer world, the outward man, who is heaven and earth, and sees and knows all diseases outside of man, if he has thereby acquired an inward image of man with all his needs, then he can turn to the inner man and be a real doctor. A doctor who recognizes the character of nature in the disease. A doctor who can translate the outside world into the inside world.

A good doctor is also an alchemist. Alchemy is a craft and like all craftsmen the alchemist completes the work of nature. The baker bakes bread, the winegrower makes wine and the weaver dyes sheets. The alchemist takes out the highest that is in nature and turns it into a medicine. The medicine must be prepared in such a way that the effect of the stars is expressed in it. The alchemist must be able to align the Mars beneath the stars with the Mars beneath the crops, so that the medicine itself becomes a star, for the stars above bring sickness and death, as well as health. Basically you take the Earth off the remedy so it can then be directed by the stars. That which belongs to Luna will be led through the stars to the brain. What belongs to the spleen will be brought to the spleen by Saturn. What belongs to the heart will be directed to the heart by Sol. The same goes for Venus and the kidneys, for Jupiter and the liver, and for Mars and the gallbladder. This also applies to all stars and there are too many to mention. Since the stars direct and not the doctor, the medicine must be brought into an air-like state. To do this, the alchemist must withdraw the four elements of the arcana. What remains is the arcanum, a kind of chaos, which can be carried by the stars like a feather in the wind. The physician must also know which star is in this arcanum, what the star of the present disease is, and thus what the star is in the medicine against the disease.

All arcana are born in the fire by one process. As the seed rots in the earth before it grows and then bears fruit, so also here, decomposition takes place in the fire. The arcana ferment there, they get rid of their matter and rise through calcination, sublimation, reverberation, solvation and so on to their higher existences and then in one more repetition the transplantation takes place. These processes take time. There is a time in the outer world and a time in man. The outer heavens also cook, conduct, imbibe, solve and reverberate. It is the course of heaven that teaches how to run and regulate the fire in the athanor (the alchemist's furnace).

For example, the properties contained in the sapphire are produced by the sky through three processes, namely, solution, coagulation and fixation. Therefore, the dissolution of the sapphire must involve these three steps in reverse order. For thus the material is separated and the arcanum remains. In this way the alchemist prepares his remedies.

The fourth pillar is the impeccable character of the doctor. He does not practice medicine out of self-interest, but in the service of others. He is not proud, does not seek profit, and does not display splendor. He is a sincere man who lives in truth and he fully masters Paracelsian medicine. He is an artist who continues to perfect his healing art. He has strong faith and accomplishes the works of God. He behaves decently and does not show off. He does not take his money to the whores.

Individuation as an antidote for cancer?

To begin with, I return to Eric Berne's three ego states: Parent, Adult, and Child.

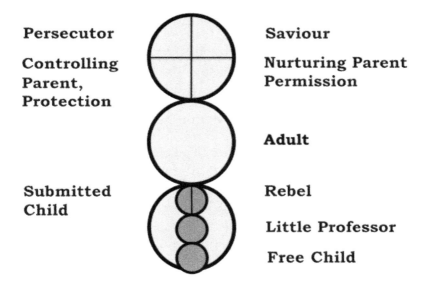

Persecutor

Controlling Parent, Protection

Saviour

Nurturing Parent Permission

Adult

Submitted Child

Rebel

Little Professor

Free Child

What we attach particular importance to, in this chapter is the Submitted Child. For whoever has an over-developed inwardly submitted child will, as I will show, be the most susceptible to cancer. Let me first delve deeper into the compliant, uncritical, unthinking, unprovoking Submitted Child who blindly follows every norm, command, measure, however foolish, unreasonable, or unethical. Submitted Children belong to the symbiotic flock of sheep that only parrot. They engage in mass crowd formation and feel at home in sectarian groups that believe in a strong leader. They follow and obey whoever has a dirty mouth. Submissive Children are part of the hypnotized mob and they believe the most foolish narrative. In addition, they tend to criticize others and betray them if necessary. They are delighted when they can take on a common enemy. It doesn't matter whether they are witches, or communists, or Jews or some non-existent virus. Submitted Children are purebred, cowardly

Nazis and collaborators. Nowadays, of course, they are jabbed and boosted. They wear face masks everywhere.

We already mentioned in the corona chronicles that the Nürnberg trials were actually a sham, where some very obedient "order-is-order potentates", who were merely part of the cogs in a mighty killing machinery, were condemned and executed, while the real evildoers, those who gave the orders, went free.

According to Mattias Desmet, this concerns 30% of the population. Milgram, who conducted his experiments on obedience at Yale University in 1963 (book 4), came to the shocking conclusion that, on average, 43% of the subjects (ordinary citizens) were willing to kill, even though it made them uncomfortable. So good, law-abiding, obedient citizens are actually life threatening. Their moral compass is not functioning, they have no backbone and they do not wish to go against any "authority" in any way. They are followers and they are believers. But they too are in danger. Because as I said, they have been vaccinated with the life-threatening syringe and there is more.

Before me lies the book entitled, "Ziekzijn: signalen van de ziel" (Sickness: Signals from the Soul) by Rüdiger Dahlke, co-author of Thorwald Dethlefsen's "De zin van ziek zijn: signalen en de betekenis van ziekten" (The Meaning of Being Sick: Signals and the Meaning of Diseases). From that book I wish to thoroughly examine the chapter on cancer. In other words, we will thoroughly examine the meaning of the clinical picture cancer.

The authors of both books assume that interpreting one's own clinical picture corresponds to working on one's own shadow (book 4), and that takes a great deal of courage. Symptoms thus invite introspection and script transformation, or in other words, personal growth. Symptoms of illness indicate that we live in a dualistic, materialistic world and that we are looking for the lost unity. Meanwhile, as integration people, we are so deeply immersed in the materialistic Baconian paradigm that there are almost no healthy people left on the planet. The earth and its inhabitants are sick.

The authors invite readers to stop getting rid of disease symptoms. The intention is to seriously decipher the syndromes, so that you can find out what they tell you. Symptoms invite you to raise your awareness, for they show that you have excluded something from your consciousness. That something then ends up in your personal shadow. For Jung, a whole person consists of a conscious I and an unconscious shadow. Together they form the self. Thus it comes down to allowing and integrating that which is unconscious into your consciousness. Jung calls this the individuation process. When you acknowledge, recognize and integrate your shadow, your conscious self grows. Now let's relate the Submitted Child as a shadow image to the predisposition to cancer.

First of all, Dahlke describes what a cancer cell is and what it does. Cancer cells simply and aggressively perform mass crowd formation. They proliferate. A cancer cell degenerates to the level of an embryonic cell and has an enormous dividing activity. In doing so, it loses its differentiated and specialized function and no longer fulfills its duties. They are degenerate, infantile cells that only reproduce. They are selfish, antisocial, boundless, unscrupulous cells that invade uninhibitedly into foreign territories. Like true parasites, they steal the nutrients and energy that healthy cells need to perform their functions. Cancer cells break out of their frame and forget everything they have learned in the course of their development. A cancerous cell is independent and does not care about its nature and function. It goes its own selfish way. It doesn't communicate. It reduces communication with the other cells to an aggressive rubbing elbows. It multiplies while employing the unethical survival-of-the-fittest philosophy.

Next, Dahlke studies the personality profile of the cancer-susceptible person, which corresponds to the Victim and the Savior in the drama triangle. Cells then appear in the body that behave like true Persecutors. Now we know from experience that Victims easily turn out to be Rescuers and that for every unit they save, Rescuers have to persecute one unit. People who have insufficiently developed their Adult and insufficiently transformed their script play all kinds of psychological games in the drama triangle, while easily fulfilling each of the three roles and switching roles.

Persecuter   Rescuer

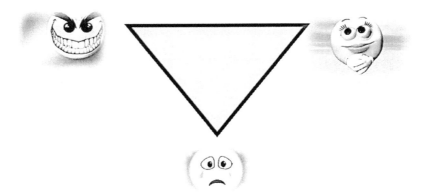

Victim

What Dahlke writes about it boils down to this. Before the cancer breaks out, we often have to deal with people who suffer from normopathy. They cling relentlessly and obstinately to the rules that prevail within the toxic structures of society. They are over-adapted, self-sacrificing gray mice, who live their lives in utter stealth. They ignore their own needs and evade all incentives that invite personal growth. New experiences are avoided. They stay in comfortable, known frames of reference (comfort zone). In stressful situations, they keep quiet and wait patiently for the unpleasant situation to pass. They don't ask questions and don't bother anyone. Tendencies to get out of hand are kept in check. They suppress their life impulses and stubbornly refuse to live their own lives. There is an unconscious latent form of depression and all attempts at rebellion are firmly suppressed. They are people who want to be good friends with everyone and who avoid conflict. They are dependent, calculable and reliable. Until now, the immune system has had a firm grip on everything in the body.

Finally, the ticking time bomb explodes and the immune system gives up. This happens after the irritation threshold is exceeded. Often it is a loss, in which a pathological grieving process is set in motion and the strong emotions of sadness, fear and anger are suppressed. Then the cancer attacks. Now two things can happen. Or the patient resignedly awaits his death, and the ego principle takes place only within his material body. Thus he consents and allows the cancer to consume him from within. Or the former modesty and proverbial tact are thrown overboard and the patient asserts himself. The peaceful, modest person suddenly demands that everything revolves around him and his illness. That is a good sign and it will mean a relief on a mental-psychological level which can somewhat temper the physical symptoms.

Nowadays we see among the jabbed and the boosted that cancers arise very quickly and metastasize all over the body in no time. We now know that the m-RNA stuff with its spike proteins destroys the immune system and then on top of that comes the ongoing stress of the unending freedom-robbing measures, while the vaccinated people were promised that life would soon return to normal. If 70% of the population were injected, it would provide herd immunity. Meanwhile, the lockdowns with the accompanying destruction of the economy continue as usual. You can imagine the deception of the fooled sheep.

There is also a spiritual component. The fact that cancer cells regress and behave like embryonic cells indicates that there is a longing for the original, paradise wholeness. On the other hand, these tumor cells, with their pursuit of omnipotence and immortality, gamble on lightning-fast progress. The cancer personality makes up for his lack of substantive significance with social success. He is kind, non-aggressive, restrained and patient, balanced and sympathetic, because he does not behave selfishly at all. He is unselfish, helpful, punctual and orderly, as well as completely rigid inwardly. All emotions and especially anger are skillfully suppressed. The cancer shows how to turn the respectable subordination ideal into the total, yet destructive, ego principle. It is as if the cancer patient is now playing the inner game in the drama triangle with body, soul and I as protagonists.

Philosophical questions such as, "who are we," "where do we come from," and "where are we going to" are expelled from the conscious mind of the cancer patient and descended into the subconscious. There they complete their work in the material body. Life has little meaning for the cancer patient. The cancer in his body urgently invites the connecting spirituality that is inherent in the quantum paradigm. The individuation process, which every Western person urgently needs and as described in the corona chronicles, is a spiritual process, where moreover, more subtle senses are developed. People would indeed better spend their energy and life force on personal development and individuation, instead of letting tumors proliferate in their bodies. But the fear of the powers and energies slumbering in each person fills the cancer personality with fear, because it invites freedom and responsibility. Self-realization means that you evolve into an autonomous, mature and self-thinking being. I.e. that the urge to expand should take place in an extension of consciousness and not in the body in the form of fanned out, aimlessly wandering cancer cells. The awareness that you consist of an immortal spiritual core with a mind-powerful purposeful I, which is connected to everything there is in the cosmos, makes the symptom of the infinitely dividing cancer cell striving for immortality completely superfluous. Because what you already know, your body doesn't have to tell you.

Now it is true that many cancer patients, when they have death in mind, search and find themselves in alternative circuits, but without being able to let go of the allopathic with its immune-destroying procedures. You can conclude that cancer sets in motion a lot of inner processes. This does not alter the fact that 50% of patients die from their cancer. You could think of cancer, like any disease, as a pathway of initiation (book 14) and we know that also in the past, not everyone completed their initiation successfully and survived the perilous ritual of will-power and focus. It didn't matter because next time, in a new incarnation, you could try again.

Ultimately, the cancer patient has to break out and break free from his self-imposed rules and procedures. He must learn to feel what he needs. He must learn to stand up for himself and his ethical values. He must dare to say resolute "no" as well as enthusiastic "yes". He must get rid of his moderate tepidity and take charge of his life with fire and flame. He has to make choices and go for it. He must know that he is part of the bigger picture and in that regard he must have a goal in mind and get his teeth into it, courageously and persistently, not shying away from any opposition. The principle of similarity from homeopathy also counts here. Cancer is an aggressive disease and should be fought with healthy aggression.

It is interesting with Dahlke to compare the psychopathic behavior of the cancer cell with the increasing imperialism and globalism in the outside world. But the cancer cells' script is self-destructive. Eventually they destroy their host and then all the cells, including the cancer cells, die. The question is whether the urge for expansion that we see in all areas -political; economically and financially- will ultimately lead to the final exit of the organism "earth", where after all it is the people themselves who represent the cancer cells. In that regard, I think we have reached a crucial stage.

February:

World Freedom Convoys, military actions in Ukraine and the Nürnberg II trials

On 4/2/22 Canadian truckers are still present in Ottawa. The population works with the local churches to feed them. They are allowed to shower at people's homes and an account has been opened to raise funds for them. They don't plan to leave until they've fully taken back their freedom and Trudeau and his gang scram. Here and there (Alberta-Montana & Ontario-Michigan) they close the borders to the US and they do so with the help of the farmers and their huge big farm machines. The mainstream media does everything it can to portray them as far-right terrorists, while it is a remarkably peaceful manifestation. The freedom fighters help and feed the homeless in the city and they have cleared the entire city of rubbish. They also clear the snow. Ottawa is now spotless. Some residents are crazy about the constant "honking". Ottawa Mayor Jim Watson ordered several companies to tow the Tow Truck Companies. But they refused and gave as an excuse that they were all at home with corona. Trudeau hides, refuses to talk to the truckers and scolds them in every way possible.

Meanwhile, the American truckers are on their way to Washington DC. Information can be found on the many telegram pages such as "US Truckers United", "USA Freedom Convoy", "World Freedom Convoy" and "Truckers For Freedom" with 10,000th followers. They report that the Facebook page of the American truckers with more than 130,000 followers were removed last week and that they will settle in a circle around Washington until the corona shit stops. Their slogan is "hunk to freedom". At Washington High School, students refuse to wear mouth diapers any longer and all day breathing their own CO2 back in. So in the US more and more people are waking up. We also read about the European Truckers going to Brussels. These more global telegram pages are more difficult to follow because there are also Spanish, Italian, German and Scandinavian messages. In addition, there is diligent twittering and new Facebook pages are springing up like mushrooms, Twitter accounts and Facebook pages are then quickly taken off the net. So it is easy to follow and report on the whole outside the mainstream media and that's exactly what I do.

The American truckers I'm currently following are calling on other truckers to join in and their route runs from Los Angeles, horizontally to California, then up the shoreline to Washington DC. New York is a little further away.

Then there is the Freedom Convoys launch in Europe and Australia. (eutimes.net/2022/01). For Europe it started in the Netherlands, Italy, France, Germany, Finland and Czechoslovakia. They leave for Brussels where they plan to arrive on 14/2/22. I see images of a convoy in Friesland, surrounded by motards. In Canada, cowboys on horseback are now also participating. Farmers with their gigantic agricultural machines join the whole. All "men with beards". It is as if the men of the world are going back into their masculine power and doing what their mission is, defending their women and children from the enemy. It seems to me to be a useful use of the necessary testosterone and I can look at that with great love.

The Australians who have suffered the most from the strictest measures are also organizing their convoys. They are on their way to Canberra. Of course, the mainstream media is silent about this in all languages.

What the mainstream press does continue to broadcast are the jingles of politicians, including Trudeau, who desperately cling to the corona narrative and continue to redirect their population towards the deadly syringe for the third or fourth time. However, a lot of people wake up and refuse the booster shots, with which they immediately lose the green tick on their QR code, get the status of unvaccinated and lose all their privileges instantly. If they end up in hospital with vaccination damage, they are of course counted among the unvaccinated. Meanwhile, alternative healers around the world are figuring out how to mitigate vaccine damage. Elsewhere (Niburu) we read that vaccinated people should continue to detoxify themselves

Yes! Groen vinkje op mijn telefoon!

In dutch we speak of a "vinkje" which means a little finch and also a tick or a mark in the shape of a flying bird. So the translation is "yes! Finally a little green finch/tick on my phone".

Notably, among the rebels there are those who fear that the whole global convoy thing is also a false flag operation sponsored by the Cabal. They fear that the store shelves will become empty, that famine will break out, that violence and riots will result, that the truckers will be blamed, that the popular anger will turn against the truckers and that the great reset will be offered as a welcome alternative. Niburu of 5/2/22 gives more explanation. The intention is to take the small independent truckers out of the economy and replace them with the self-driving e-trucks from Elon Musk. Musk has donated a large amount to the freedom convoy. Perhaps that is not as sympathetic a gesture as it seems at first glance. In the same article we read that Donald Trump also supports the spontaneous protest which is not a good sign (for those of Niburu, Trump is not trustworthy too). In the meantime, GoFundMe has stolen all donations to the truckers, because it was allegedly a violent demonstration. We are talking about about nine million dollars, which they will donate to charities. Well, we already know which "charities" such as BLM, Greenpeace, Planned Parenthood,... . So green and red charities, i.e. politic correct charities..

I do think we should have some faith in humanity and not paranoid-ally scale everything as cabalistic tactics. They're not that smart. A great new wind is blowing through humanity. Namely the conviction that it will soon be over and we already know how strong convictions can work. People are joining hands everywhere. They help each other and stand up for their point of view. They want their freedom back. It is as if the critical mass has turned and the end of fascism is in sight. All it takes is for people to stop participating, and then all this nonsense will be over immediately.

It is of course true that just demonstrating against the measures and mandatory vaccinations is not enough. Because in the end this whole corona voodoo has nothing to do with health, on the contrary. It's important to see the big picture and to know what's going on behind the scenes.

Because yes, there is an elephant in your living room and most don't even notice it.

Then we read about children who are born with big black eyes and who can do things faster than normal children. This is really creepy and maybe it's a hoax. Still, I want to go into it here, because nowadays the most craziest things happen. Niburu of 28/1/22 talks about a Mexican gynecologist (Dr. Viviane Burnet) who assumes that this is caused by the gene-mutating corona vaccines. After two days these children lift their heads, after two months they can walk and after 4.5 months they say "mama". Niburu of 4/2/22 talks about Dr. Ariyana Love who also informs us that the vaccines are genetically modifying us. She says the danger is not in the spike proteins and the graphene oxide, but that the vaccines clone us with monkeys, insects, hydras and bullfrogs. This is also what causes the disease AIDS, she says, in addition, since the vaccination there has been an increase in cancer, Ebola, all kinds of inflammation, dysfunction of the neurological system and sterility in men. It also causes dementia if it gets into the brain. The bottom line is that genes are deleted and that is an irreversible process.

That also explains the birth of children with black eyes. These babies are half human, half animal. They can run faster and all that, but they're dumber. In the end, people will thus become patentable and chipped hybrids, which will soon also have a MAC address and can be used as remotely manageable slaves via the 5G digital system. The patents of these cloned hybrids are said to be held by China and Israel. The purpose of the PCR tests would then actually be to measure to what extent humanity has already been transformed into manageable hybrids.

According to Brandon Smith (Niburu 1/2/22), the pandemic is not going smoothly. It should have become a kind of blitzkrieg where after the fear induced everyone would run to the nearest vaccination center to be genetically modified without knowing it. That's not how it went. Many people refuse to be injected. That makes the cabal distraught. Meanwhile, a number of countries are going back to the old normal, such as England, Ireland, Denmark, Sweden, Norway, Finland and Switzerland. The rather sarcastic, satirical author J.C. Hopkins (Niburu 5/2/22) thinks the covid cult is collapsing and the truckers will win. They just have to stand. Of course, it could also be that the WEF political-friends briefly dismantle the new normal before furious truckers show up at their door. And that when the storm has passed, they will start all over again. Because when the truckers occupy your capital, you have only two options: give in or use military force. With regard to the latter, the question remains on whose side the army will stand. Hopkins hopes the truckers will not give in and that the fascist leaders of Australia, Germany, Italy and France pay close attention. But whether the advancing fascism will stop completely, is the question according to donquijotte.nl, because then we might have to deal with the climate hoax or an alien invasion or Project Bluebeam, which can also maneuver us towards a NWO.

And then we finally get the formal announcement of Reiner Fuellmich's "Grand Jury - the court of public opinion". It sounds like this: A group of international lawyers and a judge are conducting criminal investigation modelled after Grand Jury proceedings in order to present to the public all available evidence of COVID-19 Crimes Against Humanity to date against "leaders, organizers, instigators and accomplices" who aided, abetted or actively participated in the formulation and execution of a common plan for a pandemic. This investigation is of the people, by the people and for the people, so YOU can be part of the jury.

Through showing a complete picture of what we are facing, including the geopolitical and historical backdrop - the proceeding is meant to create awareness about the factual collapse of the current, hijacked system and its institutions, and, as a consequence the necessity for the people themselves retaking their sovereignty. Livestream-links and more: http://www.-grand-jury.net/

So for the first time in the history of mankind, a grand jury, completely public and completely transparent to the public, on the American model, is organized outside the regular, official system, with a real judge, namely Rui Fonseca E. Castro from Portugal, with real lawyers, real experts and real witnesses. I hereby report on the first day on 5/2/22. It is a video of about one and a half hours and there are 38,370 views. The lawyers and the judge are given the opportunity to make their opening statements. As you will see, there is not much new under the sun. We actually get a summary of the corona chronicles and the evidence is on the table.

We start with lawyer Ana Garner from the USA, who explains what the intention is and how the process will go. Next, the judge, Mr. Fonseca, is introduced. He emphasizes that it is about protecting and preserving genuine democratic rights and the right to justice, as befits free democracies. People must be able to defend their fundamental rights and freedoms against any tyranny. Then it is the turn of US lawyer Deanna Sacks. She refers to the constitution from 1787. It states that medical freedom is a fundamental right. Everyone is free to decide for themselves which medical treatment they will undergo. I.e. that a government can never mandate any vaccination. Now people are being forced to take something that isn't even a vaccine, but an experimental gene-modifying drug that hasn't even been tested for what the long-term effects might be. In this case law, experts will take the floor and explain why this is not about a vaccine at all.

Then Dr. Fuellmich is given the floor. He promises to put all the puzzle pieces of this fake pandemic together to prove that this is a worldwide crime against humanity, with the sole aim of carrying out a master genocide and gaining total control over all people. There are four sets of facts that will be highlighted:

1. There is no corona pandemic, there is a PCR test pandemic, with the sole purpose of perpetuating a fear pandemic. This was accomplished by a group of psychopaths and sociopaths, who only want complete control over humanity. They use governments and media they own to spread their fear propaganda 24/7.

2. The virus itself is easy to treat with vitamins C, D, zinc etc. And also with Ivermectin and hydrochloride. However, these treatments were banned and everyone was pushed towards the ineffective and deadly vaccine.

3. The same people who were behind the swine flu plan of twelve years ago changed the definition of "pandemic" and then created panic around this so-called corona-pandemic. Also then, as now, this plan served to divert attention from

their fraudulent money practices. Because even then they were already looting the cash boxes. The governments at the time were also sold to "the other side" and it was then also the Young Global Leaders of the WEF who were in charge. Fuellmich mentions Angela Merkel and Bill Gates, among others.

4. It will be shown that the intention of the other side is to gain complete control over all of us. They do this, among other things, by destroying all SMEs, the entire retail sector as well as the tourism sector, cafes and restaurants. They also want to reduce the population to a much smaller number and they want to chip and monitor the remaining population. The mRNA experimental inoculations aim to create a trans-human breed that is microchipped and can be monitored. Furthermore, they expressly destroy democracy, the rule of law and fundamental rights through chaos. Ultimately, we must lose our national and cultural identity and accept a world government operating under the UN flag and owned by the WEF. Then a digital passport will be introduced that is linked to a digital world currency, which will be issued by a world bank.

On the dock are Drosden, Fauci, Tedros, Gates, BlackRock and Pfizer. This case concerns the crimes of a financial mafia operating in the City of London and Wall Street, who for decades planned and prepared this so-called pandemic in order to gain complete control over a decimated population. Their platform is Klaus Schwab's WEF. They meet in Davos and in China and there they make plans to realize the 2030 agenda. They started in 2001 with Operation "Dark Winter", the Lockstep exercises by the Rockefeller Foundation in 2010 and with Event 201 in 2019.

In the coming weeks a number of witnesses will be heard, such as people who have suffered damage from the so-called vaccine and those who have lost loved ones to the vaccine. There is also an undertaker from England, ex-army who took part in Operation Dark Winter, ex-members of the British secret services, investigative journalists, doctors, professors, ex-WHO and Pfizer employees. Among the experts mentioned, there are many well-known names (see the corona chronicles) such as Astrid Zuckelberg, Mike Yeadon, Dolores Cahill, our Mattias Desmond, Patrick Wood, etc. I intend to write down only what is new, because in the corona chronicles we have already discussed a lot, which should not necessarily be repeated.

Ana Garner then talks about the PCR tests. It was therefore not a "pandemic" but a "case-demic". People were led to believe that they could be sick without symptoms and that they could spread disease asymptomatically. Thus the panic was perpetuated. Healthy people were talked into being sick and the number of cases was thus pushed up to unbelievable proportions. Anyone who was sick or died with a positive PCR test was branded a corona victim, even if they had another disease or died of something else. So the numbers were cooked. The inventor of these fake tests is Drosden. This has caused a lot of damage and in that regard the necessary witnesses will be heard.

Now we hear the opening statement of the Indian lawyer Dipali Ojha. In India you have alternative and ancient ways of healing such as Ayurveda and homeopathy. Soon, these ancient and tried-and-true cures were banned from above and everyone was directed to the deadly syringe. She then explains which rules were violated according to Indian law.

Then we listen to South African lawyer Dexter L-J. Ryneveldt. He detests the so-called scientists and experts who were promoted, believed and followed by the media and the governments, because they were sold to Big Pharma and they fooled us. They were supposedly working with their proposed draconian measures in the name of the public interest, while in the end we were dealing with a common and harmless flu that was easy to treat. The lies they told will be exposed in this one. And here ends the first session of the trial.

Since we didn't talk about Dark Winter and Lockstep in the Corona chronicles, I'll say something about it here, because we find a lot of information on the internet about that. On June 22-23, 2001, about three months before 9/11, the Johns Hopkins Center for Civilian Biodefense Strategies, in conjunction with the Center for Strategic and International Studies, the

Analytic Services Institute for Homeland Security, and the Oklahoma National Memorial Institute for the Prevention of Terrorism, held a senior-level exercise titled "Dark Winter". Like the October 2019 Event 201, it was a simulation of a secret smallpox attack on the United States. The intent was to explore the challenges high-level policymakers would face if confronted with a bioterrorist attack that sparked the outbreak of a highly contagious disease in the US.

Lockstep is a pandemic scenario where the Covid-19 step-by-step plan developed in 2010 was created. The intention was to install a technocratic medical dictatorship under the guise of a pandemic. In other words, Lockstep is a blueprint of what has happened in the world over the past two years. An amplified SARS virus is being unleashed on the people, followed by a global vaccination plan, mandatory digital IDs and the indoctrination of the people through the media. Several lock-downs with curfews were envisaged, as well as impediments to freedoms such as free travel. If the people rejected the vaccinations, an even more deadly virus would then be spread. The goal was a death rate of at least thirty percent. The remaining population would live chipped and assembled in a cashless and contactless society, the NWO with all the trimmings, as there are one digital world currency, one world bank, one world religion, one world army, abolish private property, deportations to compact cities and residential areas, a Chinese-style social credit system, a ban on fossil fuels, etc. At this point, we would be about halfway through the Lockstep plan. And if the population does not wake up soon, the plan will simply be rolled out further with all the consequences that entails.

Back to the truckers of Canada. After ten days of protests, Ottawa has declared a state of emergency. The mayor (Jim Watson) talks about the most serious crisis the city has ever known. Residents complain about the constant honking and parts of the city are completely inaccessible. The police will intervene harder and block fuel and other resources intended for the demonstrators. Due to the low temperatures, the trucks' engines are constantly running so that the heating can be turned on. The demonstrators have found no better than to drive the police mad by having everyone walking around with an empty jerry can or one filled with water. Fuel is supplied via thermoses or other containers. The police, who lack sufficient manpower and do not appear to be too fanatical, in turn harass the demonstrators by issuing fines, confiscating vehicles and arresting demonstrators. The protesters hold their ground and say they will not leave until the Trudeau government resigns and the measures are abolished. The question remains whether things will escalate and the military will step in to clear Ottawa. Meanwhile, truckers are also on the road in the US and Europe.

The article about Canadian truckers in HLN is striking, come on, the news has finally reached the sold media and it is also a fairly neutral article. We read that the protest is spreading to other Canadian cities, that the chief of police (Peter Sloly) in Ottawa speaks of a siege and a threat to democracy, that farmers in Toronto, the capital of the province of Ontario, have driven to the city center, using their agricultural vehicles, that the protest is increasingly applauded, that demonstrators have also gathered in front of the parliament building of the province of Québec, that demonstrations are on the agenda in the provincial capitals of Manitoba and Saskatchewan and that the Prime Minister of the latter province also is a staunch opponent of the vaccination requirement and will announce that all measures will be lifted in his province, that the prime minister of neighboring Alberta plans to do the same, that the residents of Ottawa are tired of the occupation of their city, that 40,000 signatures have been collected for the truckers to scram, that Minister of Transport Omar Alghabra call the truckers to go home because they have made their point and everyone has heard them, that the police in Ottawa are understaffed and cannot lift the blockades on their own.

HLN of 10/2/22 reports that Belgium will ban the freedom convoys and will keep strict border controls. The reason is that no application was ever submitted. France wants to stop the convoys with heavy fines, prison sentences and heavily armed agents. That could indicate that the corrupt and sold-out governments are really afraid.

On the Vrijheidvzw.be blog we read that Michael Verstraeten, lawyer and chairman of the recently founded political party "freedom", does not agree with the way Fuellmich conducts his process outside the system. He talks about unacceptable natural law.

My own research shows that natural law is a higher and better law, based on the good order of things. In other words, it is a right based on a higher or divine principle. So it is a case law, based on morality. On the other hand, you have the positive right that was created by humans and which may well be an expression of human tyranny and violence.

Verstraeten explicitly opts for positive law and thus wants to continue to litigate within the system. He thus puts his words into action and lodges a complaint with the International Criminal Court in The Hague. He has also prepared his case down to the last detail and he submits a document of no fewer than thirty-seven A4 sheets. We'll run through it quickly. On the dock are Neil Fergusson, Head of the Infectious Diseases Department at Imperial College, London, not yet identified WHO officials, not yet identified members of the Belgian government, not yet identified members of Celeval, a Belgian advisory body, not yet identified members of the GEES, a Belgian advisory body, tot yet identified members of the Infocel, a Belgian advisory body.

They are also charged with crimes against humanity, in particular the collateral damage and collateral deaths that people have suffered as a result of the measures taken against Covid-19, a disease with a survival rate of more than 99%. Under international criminal law, you cannot commit crimes against humanity for charity or for the public interest. And crimes against humanity to fight a virus remain prosecutable.

For example, hospital beds were kept free for potential corona patients, who never showed up and other sick people were denied or postponed the necessary medical help, such as heart patients, cancer patients, diabetics, people with fractures, etc. Necessary operations were postponed with all the consequences of serve. There is also talk about the inhumane way in which the elderly in residential care homes were treated. They were isolated and all visitors were denied. They died in solitude.

Furthermore, the PCR tests that are 100% unreliable are discussed. Healthy people were thus put in sections with infected people, so that they were also infected. This also happened in hospitals. In addition, many people in hospitals were misdiagnosed with covid-19 or without covid-19, causing them to undergo wrong treatments with unforeseeable consequences. For example, people with a heart attack were mistaken for corona patients and put on a ventilator, resulting in death.

The measures also resulted in an explosion of psychological problems, such as depression and suicide. There is also the creation of a false sense of security through the non-functioning mouth mask duty. Verstraeten is also suing the CST because it has long been proven that neither the vaccines nor the boosters protect people. Then there is the damage to the economy and the dozens of small and medium-sized companies that have gone bankrupt.

The conclusion is that the Belgian governments, on the advice of the WHO, Prof. Neil Ferguson and the various advisory councils with their experts, have deliberately imposed a therapeutic experiment, without any scientific basis, on its population, without its well-informed approval and whereby several essential points of the Nuremberg Code were not respected. The result of this is very many deaths, permanent damage to the health and shortening of life of many people.

Verstraeten's indictment has been supplemented with no fewer than 15 foreign judgments, 22 press statements, 111 scientific studies, 12 publications from the WHO, 4 publications by scientists for a different policy and 32 various documents. So it is a well-founded whole. Now it remains to be seen what will happen with the charges and whether there is indeed a possibility to conduct a Nürnberg trial within the system. Personally, I have the impression that Verstraeten still thinks that it is about the health of the people and that he still does not see the fat elephant in his living room. That does not alter the fact that if he were to succeed in having a trial in The Hague, it would be quite a task in itself.

Meanwhile (12/2/22) the truckers are advancing towards Brussels, because that is where the EU, NATO and the WHO are located. It is expected that it will be a long-term action, just like in Canada. The campaign is well prepared and the entire logistics is set up. The routes are fixed, food and drink points are organized as well as fixed points where truckers can sleep and shower. People are being called upon to provide hot meals, staff the food & drink points and open their homes for truckers to sleep and shower. The English drivers have arrived at Chartres, where there is plenty of celebration. The Dutch truckers and their sympathizers are stationed in The Hague. Many roads are blocked, causing traffic disruption. It is chanted "Rutte fuck off!" There is a call to protest on 13/2/22 at the Malieveld.

Anyway, apparently our politicians already see the storm coming and they switch neatly with some relaxation from code red to code orange. Everyone cheers, because they think they can go back to the old normal. It is a relief for everyone that the mouth mask obligation for the -12 year olds is being abolished. Of course, the CST will continue to exist, as is the jabbing and boostering. Code yellow is kept as a carrot for our noses, because then there would be relaxed to zero crazy measures. But whether we can then resume our lives as before remains the question, because the media are writing us all direction a Russian invasion of Ukraine and Western citizens are being summoned to return home urgently. A war with Russia could quickly divert attention from the whole corona thing and the enormous vaccination damage, so that the politicians and their false experts do not have to end up in shame. Xander News reports that we can only hope that the Russians will stick to military targets and the "capitals of evil", which are, London, Brussels, Davos and the Vatican. In Niburu we read that Putin is also a Global New Leader and that he will play the game with Schwab. If so, we face a long stretched and grueling war on a physical, mental, emotional and spiritual level.

On 12/2/22 we also get the second session of Fuellmich's grand jury. It's a nearly six-hour session, with nearly 6,000 followers. It's about the historical and geopolitical background of the whole corona thing and they focus on a piece of history.

We are dealing with experts who go very deeply and in great detail into the matter. I rather stay on the surface and wish to make it a more readable and understandable summary.

Alex Thomson, is the first witness. He was a civil servant in the British sibling of the NSA, the spy agency GCHQ. He typed out Russian and German intercepted material. He later belonged to a team that looked into possible chemical, biological and nuclear attacks and how the Anglo-American military should deal with all matters that could potentially affect public health.

Then he talks about the dominant party in world affairs, the City of London, the financial heart of the British Empire, since 1870 and which consists of old British bloodlines (Rotschild, Rhodes...). We are talking about the industrial revolution, which went hand in hand with the installation of a political liberal democratic model and which started from the very first moment with monopolization and globalization. In that period children went to school on a larger scale and the health system as well as a legal system were set up. Dreams of a united Europe and an easy-to-manage brainwashed population were soon dreamed of. In that respect, the City of London with the Bank of England and the English church are central. These two have their own legal and political status, so that they have withstood every constitutional revolution over the past centuries. They even stood above the crown for a long time. Of course they also manage the parliaments and the political parties, who only come together, debate and make decisions, for show. Ultimately, it is these bloodlines that own and rule the British people and the British Empire and basically the whole world.

Initially, wealth was acquired through land ownership and agriculture. With the industrial revolution, money was amassed through factories and machines. This is where it becomes important to own resources and mines as well as easily manipulated human productivity (HR). Britain was far ahead of the rest of the world in that regard and for the time being there was no competition. They wanted to keep that position at all costs. They quickly colonized large parts of Asia and Africa. With the victory over Napoleon they were able to halt the socialist revolutions in Europe. They also made alliances with areas that could not be conquered, such as the Ottoman Empire. An alliance between Russia and Germany had to be avoided at all costs, so that these countries could not dominate Europe. In the chapter on Kitesh you can read what the real reason is to keep Russia away from Germany.

In addition, they wanted to contain the enormous growth in science and technology in the US and prevent the possibility of US supremacy. The US was certainly not meant to gain independence too soon. Moreover, they feared that Germany, Italy and Russia would become strong powers. There was a fight for Africa and its many mines. But Belgium and Portugal snatched large parts of Africa right in front of them. In addition, Japan became a strong state in Asia. They wanted at all costs to prevent Germany, which owned mines and grew industrially, from becoming a strong power in Europe. They made alliances with Russia and France. Those were the Allies. Germany found an ally in Italy and Austria-Hungary. That was the Centrals. They started WWI to weaken Germany and they certainly had a decisive hand in the assassination of the Archduke Franz Ferdinand of Austria.

Now the money makers of the city of London began to realize that it is also important to manage the minds of the people. They started talking about the genetic makeup of the people. The schools, the universities, the media and the English church were deployed for what is called the battle of the mind. The control of the health system was already part of this, because they wanted to possess all people completely, so in body, soul and spirit. It's about a brainwashed mind in a healthy body. If you are healthy and intelligent and educated in Oxford or Cambridge you can work for a bank, or the government or an intelligence agency like MI6. In that respect, Germany and Russia were already well advanced in conducting psy-ops.

All of the British Commonwealth and the rest of the West, through secret societies and lodges, were infected with this British worldview, which globalism already encompassed. So deep state, like a secret society, consists of these British ancient bloodlines. They consider themselves superior to the rest of the population, whom they regard as cattle and who they take for granted to manage and dominate, while successfully deceiving everyone that they live in a free and democratic world, on the Anglo-Saxon model.

Today, the heart of the financial world is even in the US, on Wall Street. Wall Street had a hand in both world events, the Bolshevik Revolution and the rise of Hitler. And in that regard I refer again to the chapter on Kitesh. There you will read how the anti-hierarchies are doing everything they can to sabotage the approaching Aquarius era and the further evolution of humanity towards socialization. They do this, among other things, by pitting Germany and Russia as enemies. That already happened in the Cold War they invented and now they are doing it again by ramping up a conflict over Ukraine.

Then we listen to the testimonies of Matthew Ehret, journalist, author and historian. He discusses the power of the English over Justin Trudeau, because according to him the Prime Minister of Canada is a stupid, hollow, lived and manipulated vessel, who has never in all his life taken his life into his own hands. We are first shown a video where Trudeau, as the best boy in the class, swears fealty to Queen Elisabeth II of England in 2017, thus revealing that as president of the so-called democratic Canada, he has nothing to say. He's Deep State's errand boy. Canada has never fought a war of independence like the US. The country was founded in 1867 and remained part of the British Commonwealth. Then we get some history about Canada which I'll skip, because I don't want to go that deep into the matter.

Interesting is the part where it is about the movement in Europe that wants to secede from the City of London and get rid of all those debts that can no longer be repaid. I suspect that this concerns the anti-globalists or the so-called populists. And more specifically I am thinking of Thierry Baudet and his Forum for Democracy in the Netherlands. I do not know to what extent our N-VA and VB share this consciousness. My question is also whether Trump is part of this movement.

Now we move on to the next presentation. We meet Brian Gerrish, a British investigative journalist and former Navy officer specializing in tracing Russian nuclear submarines during the

Cold War. He confirms that we are ruled by a group of arrogant mobsters bent on world domination. Because this is a grand jury, we have to talk about their crimes and that is repression, slavery, poverty, famine, human trafficking and murder. We are now dealing with the so-called Covid-19 pandemic and a vaccination program with the sole intention of killing people with premeditation. In the past they committed these mass murders through their created (world) wars.

Today we are fully engaged in a war of ideas and we are under a massive psychological attack. These gangsters started doing this very early, namely in 1940. And the people who were also involved at the time are now in the global mental health system. They infiltrate the world of psychological aid and psychiatric systems and conduct their propaganda there. They spread the idea of mental hygiene. I.e. that you must be fully adapted to the toxic system we live in and which was implemented by these gangsters. So psychological and psychiatric help must have the sole purpose of adapting people to society. And, I would add that they do that through behavioral therapy and chemical pills.

Furthermore, there are intelligent and well-educated people who infiltrate political systems and conduct their propaganda there. The WEF's Global Young Leaders are an example of this. Young leaders are trained to take over politics and teach people to think differently. I suspect this is about "politically correct" thinking. So left and green.

If we go back to the covid-19 pandemic we see how the psyop was run. At first people were scared. Then the people are taught to be each other's police officer. They had to persecute and betray each other. The intention was thus to provoke division and violence. This has been very successful in Australia, New Zealand and Canada.

Next, Gerrish talks about the vaccination program. The government is well aware that the number of vaccine deaths and vaccine damage is greater than the number of deaths as a result of corona. But they also know very well how to mislead the public and divert attention from the vaccine damage. And yes, I read in the newspaper that a long-term consequence of the omecron variant is heart damage and the masses believe that. According to Gerrish, it is true that it is easier to brain-wash intelligent people and that they can suffer from cognitive dissonance more than others. He urges us to be very kind and patient with these people, because they are victims and they are very damaged. When they wake up from their hypnosis they will be terribly disoriented. I add that I think he is talking about highly educated integration people with a Mephistophelic mind. Real Michaelic thinkers, with a well-functioning knowledge of discernment and who are a step further in the evolution of humanity, do not fall for this.

Then there's ex-nurse, medical examiner, and medical adviser to the government's department of health, Debbie Evens. She talks about the golden triangle: Cambridge-Oxford-London also called the brain belt. These universities study how to merge biology with technology in the name of public health, and they are sponsored by government, Big Tech, Big Pharma, major investment companies and funds like that of Bill & Melinda Gates. She says that the harmful vaccines could cause an outbreak of TB, HIV, dementia and cancer in the future and that Big Pharma together with Big tech in collaboration with these universities of the "brain belt" are already preparing "vaccines" against this.

Whitney Webb, author and investigative reporter, is the next witness. She talks about the role of China. Because until now it all seemed to be a purely Anglo-American-City of London and Wallstreet game. And it is right, because all of technocratic China with its facial recognition systems was set up with Cabal money. You could already read about it in the corona chronicles and this is confirmed here. In addition, there is Blackstone Group, an American investment company, which finances universities in China and uses it to draw out of a kind of Young Global leaders.

She then goes on to talk about Dark Winter in great detail. And I won't go into that either. This also applies to the explanation of James Bush, ex-engineer and operations manager for Infectious Disease Research Center at Colorado university, USA, who also talks extensively about Dark Winter. We just remember that back then (2001) they were already preparing a pandemic with very many victims and that the plan was to implement this in real life. Then he talks about Lockstep, a three-step approach to a permanent lockdown that results in mass depopulation.

- Step 1: a mild cold / flu —> the media induce panic —> fake PCR tests —> increase corona victims by falsifying death certificates —> obedience testing through lock-downs and draconian measures, preventing protest and identifying resistance

- Step 2: food shortages, social distancing, masks, lack of sunlight and healthy bacteria weaken the immune system —> exposure to 5G radiation further attacks the immune system —> admitting people back into society so that they get sick —> Covid-19 to blame —> induce even longer lock-downs —> start with vaccinations

- Step 3: if too many people refuse the vaccine, release an armed SARS/HIV/MERS virus on them —> many people will die —> the strongest will survive —> push everyone to get vaccinated to return to the old normal — > vaccinated will turn against unvaccinated —> with chaos as a result

by A. Ralph Epperson

These three steps can be found more or less in the 1989 book "The New World Order" written by A. Ralph Epprson. It's about how to destroy Western civilization.

On 9/18/2019, Event 201 was hosted by the John Hopkins Center for Health Security, in partnership with the WEF and the Bill & Melinda Gates Foundation. Then, a month later, the so-called corona pandemic breaks out in China. That was certainly no coincidence. Then James Bush talks about Operation Mockingbird, a CIA program that employed more than 400 journalists, not just in the US, but around the world, tasked with manipulating public opinion with propaganda and fake news, and that since 1945. He goes on to say that the BSL3 (Bio Safety Level) and BSL4 labs, where they make those amplified viruses, are growing exponentially. These labs are mainly located in the US and UK.

In between we get a movie, secretly filmed by a whistleblower, which shows how old people were injected under mental pressure from the soldiers present in a Berlin retirement home and died soon after the injection. It was pure genocide. An inquiry was requested and it was turned down. Another video is about a small demonstration that was violently stopped by a predominance of cops, because they were not wearing masks. The media never covered it.

Then there are two doctors who have worked for the WHO, Dr. Astrid Stuckelberger, international Health Scientist & Researcher, Switzerland and Dr. Sylvia Berendt, former Legal Consultant at WHO and Pandemic Manager, Austria. The latter emphasizes the fact that we are not dealing with a logical pandemic response at all. In fact, there wasn't even a pandemic, because there were virtually no cases. Drosden with his famous PCR tests caused the number of cases to suddenly increase fourteen times. She goes on to say that all the measures imposed were completely contrary to what was necessary on a scientific basis, from a health point of view, and that was the intention. Furthermore, the simulations were in no way intended as exercises for doing what is needed in a bio-attack. They were intended to be really implemented in the world and then curtail the freedoms and civil rights of the people as well as to put an incompletely approved, so-called vaccine on the market in no time. Stuckelberger adds that WHO was in cahoots with GAVI and Bill Gates and that they want to immunize the whole world, i.e. vaccinate and that's not new, they've been dreaming about that for years. And then comes the blow. The WHO is an organization that does not consist of elected people and if the WHO imposes measures, such as a lock-down, then all member states that are connected, that is all countries, must follow this measure without any explanation. That is international law and that is how the UN, in the context of their 2030 Agenda, is imposing it. Thus, private institutions and private individuals are taking over our national governments through the WHO while using public health as an excuse. Through these treaties they can impose anything on us.

Day three of the Grand Jury continues on 13/2/22 and is mainly about the fake PCR tests. It's been a five-hour session and there are now 7,250 followers. You could already read extensively in the corona chronicles about these famous PCR tests, how you can set them up and how you can manipulate them. I'll glean some news here, things that haven't been mentioned yet. Forgive me if things are repeated. For example, we hear from Astrid Stuckelberger that these tests replaced diagnoses that should have been performed by a doctor, and furthermore that there are procedures to follow in a pandemic outbreak, which were never used. No patient zero was ever designated and the virus was never isolated. She emphasizes that an effective remedy has never been found against a common cold or a flu, because the flu virus is constantly mutating, and then suddenly there is a vaccine against corona in no time. That is anything but believable. In connection with the fact that these PCR test sticks were inserted so deeply into the nose, she points out that this was already a vaccination, because that is how vets vaccinate animals. She then mentions the enormous amounts that the Charité Berlin, the institute where Drosden works, has received from GAVI. It is also said that the president of Tanzania abolished the PCR testing after it was found that a kiwi, cola, a goat and a jar of jam also tested positive. He died shortly afterwards in suspicious circumstances. Apparently this story applies to several government leaders. Nobel laureate Kary Mullis, the inventor of the PCR tests, who passed away in 2019, never invented his test for diagnosis. You can't diagnose anything with it, he said. If you multiply the samples enough, all healthy people test positive and that's what they did all the time.

Drosden, who, like our Van Ranst, advised the government as an expert and who is here on the dock, is accused of knowing full well that he had invented something to increase the number of corona cases and it was he who made the nonsense into the world as if people without symptoms would be sick and could spread a disease. Prof. dr. dr. Ulrike Kämmerer, virologist & immunologist, Germany, explains in a very scientific and detailed way what those PCR tests are and how they work. The conclusion is that on the basis of these fake PCR tests, which increased the number of corona cases, a basis was found for mass vaccination of people with a deadly vaccine, and that this is therefore premeditated genocide. Then there is the psychological damage, as people and their children are quarantined for no reason, while businesses and schools are closed.

dr. Brian Ardis, physician holistic practices and CEO of ardislabs.com, USA tells of how in 2020 at the beginning of the "pandemic" in NY clinics a respiratory virus was noticed that went to the kidneys and affected the kidneys, something they had never seen before in the treatment of flu. They complained about a shortage of ventilators and dialysis machines. What really happened is the following. Fauci ordered all people with corona in the clinics to be given remdesivir, an Ebola drug that had barely been tested and was known to be the deadliest drug in the trial. Remdesivir destroyed the organs and caused acute liver failure, heart failure and kidney failure. The doctors in NY thought that the corona virus was causing this and it was caused by the drug imposed by Fauci and the WHO. Hydroxy chloroquine and chloroquine were banned. The US and Brazil are the two countries with the highest mortality from Covid-19 and both countries treated their corona patients with remdesivir. He then goes on to tell how in the UK in March 2020, 18,000 and in April 2020, 25,000 old people were killed in care facilities with morphine and midazolam (an opiate). They were all presented to the press as covid-19 casualties. I heard the same story on a David Icke videocast last year. Icke also claimed that they did this in the US as well. So again we can speak of genocide with premeditation. Then Dr. Ardis presents the evidence.

The next witness is John O'Looney, funeral director who determined no excess mortality in 2020. He did see a lot of edema in the abdominal area and the lungs during embalming. Everyone had a covid-19 death certificate, even if you could tell they had just had heart surgery, eg mass vaccination started on 6/1/21 in the UK. He thought the death toll would drop, but to his surprise, it rose by 300%. Then they started with a new badge or something and it got less. He has dealt with many young people who had died of a thrombosis, inflammation of the heart muscle or a heart attack. A doctor friend who works in a hospital told him that the death rate there had increased by 600% by 2021 and that many died of thrombosis.

Then Dr Shankara Chetty, General Practitioner, South Africa takes the floor. He talks about how he initially observed this entire corona pandemic with great suspicion. And with his story you really wonder whether he is really the only allopathically trained doctor in the world who quickly realized that something was absolutely wrong. He initially thought it was highly suspicious that the Chinese virus was spreading all over the world and as far as China is concerned, it only stayed in Wuhan. He was also very concerned about these PCR tests because he knew they were not intended to diagnose. In all his training and his experiences as a doctor, he had never heard of the asymptomatic spread of a disease. Then came the mask duty and he knew very well that masks don't stop viruses. Then came the measures that wanted to isolate people for a fortnight and he saw that there was no scientific basis whatsoever for all these measures. Furthermore, the doctors were not allowed to meet the patients, they had to tele-diagnose and if necessary refer the people to a hospital.

Then the pandemic descended to Italy, where many people suffered from corona and died. Doctors made reports of their diagnoses and these could thus be studied. What was very unusual was the loss of smell and taste and of course the shortness of breath. With these symptoms he immediately thought of hydroxy chloroquine, because he had had good results with it for years and he kept it in stock. The next day, the drug was banned by the government and taken off the shelves.

When the pandemic hit South Africa, he decided to see and investigate every patient in person. He came to the conclusion that almost all of his patients had a simple flu, with all its symptoms, and that most recovered without much effort within a few days (two to five). When the symptoms were severe, they were given hydroxy chloroquine. He did, however, urge the patients that if they had trouble breathing, they should come back immediately. Ultimately, there were a number of patients who returned with respiratory distress. The day before they were completely healthy and it always came exactly one week after the first symptoms (sore throat). So something new happened. There were two illnesses at work, which had nothing to do with each other. Dr. Chetty suspected that these people must be allergic to something and gave them an antihistamine, which gave good results. That's why he thinks this "pandemic" is all about a lab-boosted virus and that people prone to allergies are reacting to the unnatural spike proteins. As a doctor, he has not lost a single patient to this pandemic. He decided to write a paper about it and send it to all involved (doctors and patients, including through the media). There he met resistance. I think that the doctors are the same as the journalists. They don't investigate anything, they don't think for themselves, they just copy-paste, follow the rules and do what is imposed on them from above. Moreover, if the previously symptom-suppressing allopathic physicians were on par with Dr. Chetty, developing a vaccine would have been completely unnecessary.

There is not much news about the convoy to Belgium. The city center of Brussels was cordoned off with containers on 14/2/22 and operation snail on 15/2/22 didn't get much done. The images of the Brussels ring road show the normal, daily traffic jams, which of course also include trucks. We see no flying colors, no bells and no whistles. The people who had provided food for the truckers were left with their supplies.

On 15/2/22 we read in HLN that in Canada, Trudeau is calling on the emergency act to end the trucker protests. That is, he can do anything without being held accountable, such as blocking accounts of alleged terrorists, seizing private property, imposing fines, or putting people in jail for no reason. He wants to block the truckers' accounts and cancel their vehicle insurance policies. Fortunately Trudeau does not have the support of the full parliament, the Prime Ministers of Alberta, Manitoba and Saskatchewan are opposing Trudeau's decision to invoke the emergency law against the truckers and will not allow it on their territories. The result is a so-called "bank run". Canadians get their money from the banks en masse. Meanwhile, the organizers of the freedom convoy are arrested. This news can be found in Niburu and Xander Nieuws of 18/2 as well as on the telegram pages of the truckers for freedom. There I also read that demonstrators in Australia were attacked by the police with EMF weapons and that people suffered severe burns as a result. On 19/2/22 it happens. In Ottawa, the NWO army is deployed en masse and there is disproportionate crackdown on the peace-loving demonstrators. The soldiers are not Canadians, they do not speak English, they are masked and do not wear badges. Trudeau wins this battle, but his reputation as an empathetic leader is completely ruined.

On 19/2/22 there is the fourth session of the grand jury, which is about the injections. The whole thing takes almost six hours and there are now 10,000 followers. We start with two videos. In the first, Bill Gates is speaking. His body language is remarkable. He's all huddled up and holding himself tight. He constantly puts his hand to his mouth which indicates that he is lying. I remember that they made more vaccines than there was demand, the vaccines did their job, and next time they will get their vaccines to market even faster. The second film is about a woman who, after the injection, becomes paralyzed in her left arm, suffers constant pain and lost her job due to frequent absences.

Then Dr Alexandra Henrion Caude, director of research in genetics, has the floor. She shows a number of slides from which we can deduce the following. In the past year, 3.3 million side effects of the vaccine were recorded in the WHO's VigiAccess database, including many deaths. There were ten times more deaths from vaccines last year than we have experienced in the past 50 years. In the vaccination death statistics, Israel leads the way, followed by the US, Italy, Sweden, Mexico, UK, Brazil and South Africa. India and Africa have the fewest vaccine deaths. However, in all countries the curve is going up and for Israel, where the fourth injection was massively put, that is exponential. For Dr Alexandra, the covid-19 vaccines are ill-considered and unethical as they are still in the research and development stage. The tests always showed that the mRNA vaccines did not work and that they caused mutations and other things that are dangerous for the body. In addition, they knew that these vaccines repeatedly boost the body and thus over-stimulate their host's immune system. The vaccines were presented with false and ever-changing promises, due to the fact that they are still in a clinical trial period (until 2023). The syringes have not ended the pandemic, they have not eliminated the virus and they have not protected anyone from the disease, as new variants keep appearing. The immune status of the people was not taken into account, because those who had had corona were also vaccinated, which is absolutely unnecessary and even dangerous. All other treatments were excluded (ivermectin and chloroquine). There was no serious assessment of epidemic dynamics and no pharmacovigilance. The risk-benefit analysis left much to be desired. The result of the vaccinations was a huge excess mortality in 2021. We are facing an unprecedented global situation where a few people (three million so far) were injured and where all vaccinated people are potentially at risk as well as the next generations, and that does not outweigh the the few benefits. The conclusion is therefore that vaccination must stop immediately.

The next expert is Dr. Vannessa Schmidt-Krüger, molecular biologist, specialist in cardiovascular diseases, Germany. She says that everyone already had a strong immunity against corona viruses and their variants and that vaccination was therefore completely unnecessary. Moreover, there is no need at all for an mRNA vaccine. No one dies from corona viruses, she says, people die from underlying conditions and a weak immune system. The vaccines are thus completely useless and, moreover, they do not work.

Then comes Canadian immunologist and psychologist Deanna McLeod, who has spent more than 2,000 hours researching Covid-related clinical data with her team since March 2020. Her conclusion is that the Pfizer inoculations do more harm than good. She proves this to a number of transparencies with a detailed explanation and concludes that the vaccination must stop immediately.

Then we get the testimony of Prof. Dr. Sucharit Bhakdi, micro-biologist, immunologist and infection epidemiologist from Germany. He says that if during a trial period, which we are now in the midst of, there is a clear indication that the drug in question is causing illness or death, then the experiment should stop immediately and that is clearly happening in hundreds of thousands of cases now. These so-called vaccines have two toxic components, namely the fat package, which has never been tested on an animal or human body, and the virus itself, which encodes spike proteins. If your own body cells start to produce spikes and release them in the body, that is toxic. Your own body will therefore produce that poison itself. Then these cells, which produce the spikes, are attacked by the immune system.

The spikes are injected into the arm muscle and then they go into the bloodstream through the lymph nodes. This was just predictable and doctors need to know that, it's basic medicine. The spikes damage the veins, which then leak and the spikes end up in the tissue of the organs. There they are attacked by the immune system. Thus tissue everywhere is damaged by the spikes and then by the immune system. Blood clots form, in the brain, or the heart, or anywhere. Fifty percent of people who got their second shot complain of headaches. That's because clots form in the brain. People become blind, or deaf, or paralyzed. Psychological changes are also noted in vaccinated people. Their personality changes. Their humanity changes. Others get Alzheimer's. It's awful. The vaccines also kill cells in the lymph nodes. Lymph nodes protect you from infections. That increases the risk of TB. Cancer cells will also no longer be kept in check. There is an explosion of tumors among the vaccinated. These vaccines are of no benefit and they can kill you and your children in a thousand ways. In the meantime, everything he says has been published, so whoever cooperates for a second is guilty of first-degree murder. He hopes that as all this comes to light, the value of Pfizer's stock will fall below zero and lead to total bankruptcy.

Then we hear Mike Yeadon. He spent 33 years in the biopharmaceutical industry as a biologist, immunologist and toxicologist. He worked for Pfizer as chief scientist and vice president of pulmonary research in the UK and US. He begins by saying that these vaccines are very bad products, that it is absolutely unnecessary to get vaccinated, especially not for a flu with such a low mortality. In fact, he's only just figuring out that if you want to make a vaccine for any pandemic that's safe, the pandemic will be over long before you have your vaccine ready. What we see now is a fake vaccine, which is poorly developed and poorly designed. These vaccines have never worked, and even if they were safe, they might not work. These vaccines were created to make money and to maneuver people into that digital passport, which in turn should lead to total control. It's also a form of mind control, because they trick people into thinking it's about legit products and they will definitely make and re-use them. However, they are not vaccines at all and in the meantime they have been proven to be harmful. Moreover, these so-called vaccines are designed to be poisonous, because they are made by very smart people, who knew beforehand what they were doing. They were fiddling with spikes, which are genetically unstable and very similar to human spikes and that makes the chance of autoimmunity huge. In addition, it is not known for how long the body will produce these poisonous spikes, nor in which part of the body it will occur. In addition, it is absolutely impossible to make large numbers (millions and millions of doses) of this product in such a way that all products are identical. So there are huge differences between the batches and the syringes. There's a wide variety of toxicity and you really don't know what you're going to get into your body when you take the vaccine.

According to Yeadon, there is a very high level of criminal conspiracy and fraud. The fact that they want to vaccinate the entire planet has absolutely nothing to do with health and it has to do with control. Because there are a large number of people that you certainly don't need to vaccinate, and those are the people who have recovered from the disease, because they are already immune. They will have hyper-immune reactions and become very sick. The pandemic has now been going on for two years. There is no longer a pandemic and everyone is now immune. Vaccinating children is also a crime, it only harms them and that is also the case for pregnant women. If you are going to vaccinate pregnant women, you know in advance that it has nothing to do with public health. The same is true with boosters. It is absolutely completely inadequate to vaccinate people multiple times. If that happens, you are dealing with fraud. It is clear as a rock that we are dealing here with intentional crime. Both Pfizer, and Johnson and Johnson and Astra Zeneca and all the others, knew very well what they were doing.

Then we get Prof. Dr. Arne Burkhardt, pathologist, Germany. He tells what they learned from about thirty autopsies and four biospies. It concerns men and women who died between seven days and six months after their last injection and who were between 28 and 95 years of age. They received vaccines from Pfizer, Moderna, Janssen and Astra Zeneca. They found damaged veins as well as damage to the lungs, heart, brain, spleen and lymph nodes. Sometimes they also found the spikes in the tissue. Under the microscope you could see severely damaged cells. This thus confirms Dr. Bhakdi's story.

Nano-pathologist, founder of free health academy, Italy, Prof. Dr. Antonietta Gatti then takes the floor. She is talking about the nano-technological aspects of these products, because they are not vaccines. Our immune system does not respond to these nanoparticles. Because her English in Italian is not understandable, I refer to what was previously written about nano-technology in the so-called vaccines in the corona chronicles.

Prof. dr. Werner Bergholz, professor of electrical engineering, Germany, taught quality and risk management at the university. In his presentation he summarizes what we have heard so far. He says that the development process was very flawed and that urgency can certainly not be an excuse. There was certainly no stable mass production which made the batches differ enormously from each other and that very lethal batches were produced. As a result, we now have a pandemic of the vaccinated. In Germany, between 2,000 and 2019, you have about 20 deaths for about 70 million vaccinations. Now there are 2,255 deaths per year from about 140 million injections. That's fifty times more deaths per injection. This is confirmed by VAERS and official statistics in other countries. Next to spikes, graphene oxide has also been detected in the vaccines. In addition, metal objects and fragments of microchips have been found in the vaccines. It could be that this comes from censors in the production process.

Several studies conclude that the deaths are related to the spike production in the various organs. This can occur just after or months after the injection. No one knows how much, where and for how long the spike production continues in the body. Every organ and every function in the body can be affected. His conclusion is that the production of all vaccines should be stopped and that a serious investigation should be started. All the rules of what we call "total quality management" (TQM) were broken by the vaccine manufacturers.

The next expert to testify is Meredith Miller, coach and author. She talks about the psychological effects of psyops and how to recognize the red flag around emotional abuse. For this she relies on a study from Yale University in 2020, which is specifically about the manipulation techniques that are used today. The first symptom she wants to discuss is the cognitive dissonance, which is phase one. When people believe the plandemic narrative and you then give them evidence and facts of what's really going on, there's an internal conflict in the brain. That induces a lot of stress and anxiety in the nervous system. The brain is kidnapped and the person goes into denial (don't know). Today these people are confronted with a lot of evidence to the contrary of what they have been told and that makes them angry with the messengers. They remain in a kind of brain fog and they only want to see the good in the perpetrators. Then comes phase two. People start to isolate themselves (physically or mentally). This was further reinforced by the government by imposing the lock downs and quarantines.

(I would add that the 2021 film "Don't Look Up" starring Leonardo DiCaprio, Meryl Streep, Jennifer Lawrence and Cate Blanchet provides a great example of denial.) The victims don't want to know what is really going on and stick to the perpetrator's narrative. Over time, the victim's neurological system begins to change. They can no longer maintain social ties and may even react aggressively if given a chance to socialize. They disconnect completely and then start to feel unsafe. While they are isolated at home, they do have their TV, cell phone and internet on, which feeds them again and again with the lies surrounding the so-called pandemic. When they sit on the bus or go to the supermarket, they are constantly told the same messages over the loudspeakers, namely that they should wear their masks and get vaccinated.

Stage three in abusive situations is that the victim is torn between idealizing and devaluing the abuser. The perpetrator does this by rewarding and punishing them. Thus, moments of relaxation alternate with moments of severe stress. The government does this by imposing increasingly strict measures and then abolishing them. Vaccinated people are rewarded with privileges, called freedoms, which are subsequently revoked. As a result, the victim will work harder to get the reward. He almost develops an obsession to satisfy by following the most absurd rules. He becomes addicted to the hope of a reward.

Now we see a number of countries abolishing all measures and people hope that they can finally go back to the old normal. They relax. However, the perpetrator doses his kindness, you get little bits of it. Governments are also releasing little bits of the truth so that those who don't believe in the narrative can also have hope in the end of the whole madness.

The next stage is even more serious. After frequent bombardments of fear, the autonomic nervous system starts to perceive things as life-threatening. The result is that the victim enters a freezing mode, a trauma cramp (book 1), he goes into shock and he exits. The metabolism breaks down and his immunity drops. Now we have two types of victims. On the one hand you have the people who are afraid of the virus and of the other people who can be spreaders because they are not vaccinated or do not wear a mask. On the other hand, there are the people who are afraid of the upcoming fascism and the NWO. Both feel there is no way out, they are immobile and in a state of shock. They feel powerless, they lose control and they become exhausted. They no longer have the energy to fight or stand up for their rights. They are in a basic state of consciousness and are no longer able to use their thinking or their imagination or their creativity. They spend their entire lives on autopilot. They go to work, take their kids to school, run errands, etc. And then they go home again. There is no hope for a future anymore. They become completely empty inside and that is the worst thing that can happen to a person. People flee into fantasy. We are seeing an increase in all forms of addiction, such as pornography, drugs and also suicide. When people are that far, awakening is impossible. They end up taking the vaccine because they want it to be over and that was the whole point of this psyop. This explains why victims of abusers are irrationally loyal to the perpetrators and do not want to see the truth.

Ultimately, the goal of this psyop was that people would not only take the vaccine, but also convince others to take it, because whoever is not vaccinated is antisocial, selfish, dangerous, cowardly, untrustworthy and he has no believe in science. Debt induction was key here.

After this psychological eye-opener, Dr. Ariane Bilheran, clinical psychologist and author from France, speaks. She specializes in all forms of abuse, oppression, manipulation, bullying, intimidation, paranoia and totalitarianism. She elaborates on the matter. She claims that we are dealing with a totalitarian current based on paranoia. This is a form of psychopathy that involves intimidation, manipulation, guilt induction, and all forms of psychological, mental and physical violence. The structure is always the same. There is the delusion that a war must be waged against an existing or nonexistent enemy, in order to eventually regain the lost paradise. That justifies the use of all possible means of power to achieve the goal. In a totalitarian context, the content of the delusion can change. This allows the designated enemy to alternate. It doesn't matter if it's a virus or Jews or communists. The structure remains the same.

An unabated moral pressure is exerted on the people. The people live under a constant state of terror, which greatly reduces the mental health of them. We speak of depression, suicide, psychological disorganization, addictions, confusion, psychiatric decompensation and schizophrenia. Children and young adolescents in particular suffer from this. In 2021 there was a serious increase in suicides in that age group in Paris. Then there are the psychosomatic disorders.

All legal, moral and spiritual boundaries are crossed. Individuals must make sacrifices in the name of the common good. Human rights are abolished. For example, children are denied the right to education. Another example is that health care providers must be vaccinated. Another sacrifice lies in the breakdown of the economy that has left countless people in poverty.

The initiation of totalitarianism always starts with fear induction and guilt induction along with taking away fundamental freedoms as has been done by lock downs and quarantines from the beginning. Anyone who does not follow the measures is a murderer. In Italy, when traveling by train, you had compartments for the vaccinated and compartments for the unvaccinated. Unvaccinated people were denied essential care in hospitals and children were made to believe they were responsible for their grandmother's death. People are presented with false choices such as whether you get vaccinated or you can no longer work. Meanwhile, the hypnotic suggestion continues through the media, further perpetuating the panic. Another feature is censorship and prosecutions, as well as intimidation and blackmail.

People are again and again brought into a traumatic shock state by last minute imposed heavy measures or by contradictory measures. Civilians are treated like prisoners, but they have gone into a traumatic dissociation and no longer see how dangerous and violent the government really is. The manipulations by the government and the mass media have led to divisions in families, couples, colleagues and circles of friends. Society was divided into two camps under the motto divide and rule. In addition, people were reduced to a number or a positive or negative tested case.

What is happening now is reminiscent of how cults work. People also have to believe blindly and do not analyze anything critically. It is an ideology reminiscent of fetishism and the holy grail is the syringe that will deliver us from all evil. For in a totalitarian state, a promise is kept like a carrot in front of the believers. The aim is to achieve an idealized context, a paradisiacal situation, without Jews or communists or life-threatening viruses. To achieve that, sacrifices must be made and the people must suffer.

The perpetrator who suffers from paranoia knows that he is harming people and he condones this because everything is supposedly done in the public interest. The people are his enemies and there are too many of them. They must be eliminated in a eugenic way. The means is to induce a mass psychosis, because eventually the NWO's must have a number of people completely alienated from themselves and the others who they can use as slaves.

On 20/2/22 we have the fifth session of the grand jury. It is about the financial destruction of our society. This session lasts about four and a half hours and there are now 11,000 followers. After the judge's usual summary, we move on to the testimony of Patrick Wood, economist and author. We already know him from book 13, where we talked about technocracy. He gives a geopolitical background and starts with the statement made at the Davos meeting on 24/1/20 by Marc Benioff, namely that capitalism as we have known it is dead. At the same meeting, Angela Merkel said that capitalism is the worst of all possible economic systems. On 30/1/20, the WHO declares that public health is an international matter. And that's where the pandemic actually started. However, the ideas about installing the NWO already started to emerge in the early 1970s. The initiators were the Rockefellers and the UN. In 1992, in a meeting that took place in Rio De Janeiro, the UN adopts the 2021 agenda in the context of sustainable development goals. In 2000 the UN met in New York where they worked out eight Millennium Development Goals. In 2015, the UN met in Addis Ababa and created the 2030 Agenda with its seventeen sustainable goals. We already discussed these agendas extensively in the corona chronicles. Also in 2015, there was a Christiana Figueres, Executive Secretary of the UN Framework Convention on Climate Change, who said it is the first time in human history that we set ourselves the task of changing, within a certain period of time, the model of economic development that has dominated us since the industrial revolution for one hundred and fifty years. So "sustainable development" is the high word here in the dictionary of the news speech of the men of the NWO, but they mean something different than us. And that is in one word: technocracy à la China, with digital coins and total control no privacy and no private property. This is not compatible with capitalism, so capitalism has to be killed in the following way and they are in full swing right now.

○ Withdrawal of energy

○ Withdrawing resources and creating shortages

○ Sabotaging the supply chains

○ Withdrawal from labor

○ Withdrawal of capital

○ Limiting consumption (introducing poverty)

○ Limiting innovation

○ Creating catastrophic events —> fear —> isolation

○ Creating Bad Investments

Then comes Schwab with his Great Reset and his famous phrase, "you will have nothing and be happy".

Next, Wood gives a definition of "technocracy". It is the science of social engineering, the scientific operation of the total social mechanism to produce and distribute goods and services for the total population. There is no place for politics, politicians, finance, financiers. ... Technocracy will distribute on the basis of a distribution certificate available to every citizen from birth to death (From 1938 "The Technocrat" magazine). For the WEF and the UN, technocracy is the only alternative economic system in the history of the world. And in order to install it, everything that has been built up to this point must first be destroyed. The NWO can then be built up from scratch. That's what they mean by "build back better". You can read more about Wood and technocracy in book 13. Wood ends his speech with this picture.

The image above is from the 1930s. I suspect if you zoom out in your mind you will see Lord Michael's foot somewhere on the dragon's back. That is, if we humans join the legions of this warring zeitgeist. And with the peace-loving freedom convoys moving around the world today, bringing with them a great awakening, I think we're well on our way. Because these truckers, along with the residents of Ottawa, are doing exactly what people do. They dance in the streets, they celebrate, they hug each other, they take care of the homeless, they clean the streets, they are polite and loving and despite all the provocations, they remain peaceful.

After this, we are shown a two-minute video where Christopher Cole, FDA Executive Officer of Countermeasures Initiative, speaks. (The FDA is the body responsible for protecting public health by ensuring the safety and efficacy of human and veterinary drugs, biologics, and medical devices.) He says Biden wants as many people as possible to get the injections. Plus, Big Pharma, Big Food and vaccine manufacturers pay them hundreds of millions of dollars a year to approve their products. Now they want to maneuver everyone towards an annual vaccination. They will gradually introduce this annual vaccination obligation through the schools. Ultimately, that will also apply to the toddlers, and that while the testing process is not yet complete and you cannot assure the parents that it is one hundred percent safe.

Then we get another movie where the WEF presents the internet of bodies. With a smile, the whole thing is sold as an ecosystem monitored by an AI, which collects personal health data and can change bodily functions. Everyone will be monitored in every aspect of their life, that is what you eat, what you buy on the internet, how much energy you consume, how you handle your health and how healthy you are, how you are genetically composed, how it is about your mental health, how you behave, how you grow old, etc.

The next expert speaking is Lesley Manookian, Former Investment Banker & president of the Health Freedom Defense Fund, USA. She knows how things work in the business world and she talks about it. Her conclusion is that under the guise of fighting a pandemic, we are currently dealing with an intentional demolition of our political and economic system so that they can restart it according to their own taste. They only care about money, power and control.

As an investment manager, she experienced the following. Investment managers always agree with management. They don't give feedback, they don't discuss and they don't complain. But if they don't agree with management, they just sell their shares. That's the opposite of what you learn in business school.

She then explains how high-level management teams think. For example, in a large pharmaceutical company was leaked that a number of people had died while testing a drug. This was not disclosed and discussed with the investors. They were simply told that everything was fine and that millions would be made on the drug nonetheless. For her, this was the sign that despite the fact that she had a great career, she urgently needed to get out of this world.

It's important that you understand the context above, she says, so you can apply it to what's happening right now. These are people without a moral code. They live in luxury while they want to enslave the rest of the people.

According to her, their crime in this grand jury is the deliberate destruction of Western civilization. Then she talks about the motive. Since things were already going bad in the financial world, it was necessary to build a parallel system, and they have been working on that for decades. Now we are in the midst of a rapid acceleration. The "question why now?" and "why us?" is answered as follows.

According to her, their crime in this grand jury is the deliberate destruction of Western civilization. Then she talks about the motive. Since things were already going bad in the financial world, it was necessary to build a parallel system, and they have been working on that for decades. Now we are in the midst of a rapid acceleration. The "question why now?" and "why us?" is answered as follows.

The financial crisis started in 2008-2009, when US government debt exploded. A few years later, the pension crisis exploded. This was due to low to negative interest rates (since 2014). Those who invest do so because of the interest it generates. If there is no interest, nothing is earned. Public pension funds generally invest in government bonds. If these yield nothing or are even negative, then you will have problems, because the state pension funds must yield about 8% per year in order to survive and pay the retired civil servants. In concrete terms, this means that there was no more money to pay out the pensions. Imagine if people would discover this. Then you get lynchings. Therefore, the entire system had to be rebooted quickly. This is not only true for the US, but also for Europe, the UK, Australia, Canada, Japan and around the world. We must not forget that all those huge amounts of debt, which run into the trillions, and which are created out of thin air, do end up in someone's pockets. And that it is the taxpayers who pay.

In October 2019, there was another banking crisis. The money was only worth 10% back then, which is next to nothing. So something had to be done very quickly. And here you have the motive for the great reset, where all debts would be forgiven and at the same time you would own nothing and be happy. In other words your property is simply taken over by the 1%. Because of course there is always someone who does own the possessions. Everyone would receive a universal basic income, and that via a digital currency, issued by one central world bank. This is also the reason why all those small businesses, which make up the largest part of the economy, urgently need to be destroyed. And that is exactly what they are doing through all those measures.

Then she talks about total medical control, which is also an important component in this whole thing. It's about Big Pharma, the hospitals, the NGOs, the research institutions, the national and international health organizations, the big foundations like that of Bill & Melinda Gates, George Soros and the Rockefellers. The latter sponsor schools and universities, research institutes, the media and politicians. They dictate, censor and thus control everything that is said, written, published and taught, including the items concerning health and disease. The result is that you cannot trust your own doctor, because he too has been brainwashed by this mafia.

She then briefly discusses how this total control will take place. She talks about Elon Musk's Starlink, the internet of some 1,700 satellites. Bill Gates' EarthNow, with some 500 satellites; 5G and the Internet of Things and the Internet of Bodies. She also briefly talks about vaccination passports, ID 2020, nanotechnology, microchip implants, mind control, etc., all things that were frequently reported in the corona chronicles.

She also says that the 1% now has their backs against the wall. Too many people are awake. They can no longer maintain that it is about health and certainly not after what we have seen in Canada. The people there are waking up en masse and there is an excess of violence. This makes it abundantly clear that it is about control and not about health at all.

In between we get a testimony from South African Benita Black, a victim of the Pfizer vaccine. She is shaking and trembling, as we have already seen in many videos on Facebook.

Then we move on to the financial component with Björn Pirrwitz, lawyer and financial expert, Germany. Today, he says, we see a completely different form of shareholder activity, under the name of corporate social responsibility. All shareholders participate in this. That was certainly sarcastic, because I think CSR, which means that an organization is responsible for the effects of its decisions and activities on society and the environment through transparent and ethical behavior, is another word in the dictionary of the Newspeach of the NWO. And rest assured that they mean and do just the opposite.

Pirrwitz will talk about the money system and how to create money out of thin air. There are two major milestones. The first is the decoupling of money from the gold standard by Nixon and the creation of fiat money in 1971. The too expensive war in Vietnam is said to have played a part in this. Since then, the monetary value has been based on the trust of the people. When the trust is gone, the money is worth nothing. The second milestone is the 1986 big bang in the London Stock Exchange, which Margaret Thatcher was behind. From then on, banks were allowed to do whatever they wanted. This led to a huge stock market rally and the dot com bubble (1995-2001). The values of shares in internet companies rose enormously as a result of the (expected) growth of these companies. This is where casino capitalism started. I.e. that large global capital flows are constantly on their way to places with the highest possible returns, regardless of the negative impact on society. This made the markets highly volatile and unstable, leading to the massive economic and financial crisis of 2008.

Till today we are dealing with an unresolved global financial crisis from 2007-09. Bad assets were moved from the bank balance sheets to the central banks, who stood surety and had the only way out to print even more money. This led to the destruction of the banks' earnings model via negative interest rates, resulting in asset inflation. The printed money has gone straight to the investors, but it is no longer worth anything.

We have now reached a point where there are no more resources and there is no way out, because printing even more money is no longer an option. The collapse of the financial system is inevitable and it will happen when the people realize that the emperor wears no clothes. When trust in the system disappears, there is no more system. Then there will be a bank run and then it's done. That's what they want to avoid at all costs. They have their backs against the wall and their only way out is the great reset with all the trimmings, as we have already discussed several times. Björn Pirrwitz recommends taking all your money out of the bank before a massive bank run, because then you will lose everything.

This argument is supplemented by the explanation of the economist, Prof. Dr. Christian Kreiss, who sees things from a different point of view and who will focus on solutions. He will talk about rising inequality and its consequences. He points out that since the 1970s, the productivity of the working population has increased enormously and wages have not increased accordingly. Now, if you're getting $7.25 an hour, which is the minimum wage, you should actually be making $26 if you convert it. And that also applies to Europe and all industrialized countries. The surplus goes of course to the 1%. But that way you narrow your sales market, so the supply exceeds the demand. Still, initially enough was sold because people started buying things on installment and thus a lot of debts were incurred. The debt burden thus rose exponentially and for Kreiss that is the cause of the financial crisis, because if the debt burden goes up, it has to be kept up by printing more money. So Kreiss speaks here not only of the indebtedness of governments, but of private individuals. The debt burden is now so high that it can never be repaid. At this point there are three possible solutions and they are inflation; a financial crisis, depression and deflation; and war. This time a plandemic was chosen.

The richest in the world always make more money during a crisis or a war, because then they can eliminate the competitors. The lockdowns have brought in a lot of money for the big players like Amazon, while the small players have been systematically eliminated. This pandemic was easy to induce because the 1% own the governments and the media. Thus they could mislead and hypnotize the people through fear. In times of crisis, cash is always king. The 1% own large amounts of cash reserves. Kreiss shows that the richest in the world have become even richer during this so-called pandemic crisis. In fact, they have never been so rich.

Nice is that at the end Kreiss refers to Rudolf Steiner, and Goethe's Faust. Steiner warned in 2017 that the ultimate goal of the elite is to take away the freedom of the people. And now we see how easily people exchange their freedom for (false) security. I will not go too deeply into what Kreis says about Steiner and Goethe's Mefisto, because enough has already been said about it in the corona chronicles. In any case, my heart jumps when it turns out that Fuellmich's panel talks about spirituality and about Steiner predicting that vaccines will be used in the future to cut people off from their spirituality. Kreis also speaks - without mentioning it explicitly - about the danger of the Azural shadow, where children are taught through games to kill without empathy and without humanity. Kreiss concludes that the 1% is not even about money or power or control, but about destroying ethics (the good order of things), destroying spirituality and destroying humanity. We are taken over by Mefisto.

Then Kreiss talks about the solution and that is, consciousness, consciousness, consciousness. People need to wake up. We have to decentralize and establish our own free press, our own schools, etc. And yes, we have already talked about that in the corona chronicles. Then Kreiss talks about Steiner's threefold society, which you can read about in book 14. The fifth day of the grand jury ends with the saying: "be the change you want to see in the world".

Now let's go back to the Ukraine debacle for a moment. In Niburu 22/2/22 we read that Donetsk and Luhansk which are in eastern Ukraine have declared themselves independent republics. Russia recognizes these mini-states from the Donets basin (Donbass) and is now going to send peacekeepers there. For the rest of the world, that means Russia with its troops is violating Ukraine's territory and they will most likely consider this an invasion. For example, in the sewer magazine AD.nl we read about the parts of Donesk and Luhansk occupied by the separatists. The inhabitants of these two countries, about 720,000 people, speak Russian and are hated by the Ukrainians.

A bit of background information might be in order here. It comes from Xander News of 23/2/22. I summarize briefly. In 2019, Volodymyr Zelensky was elected by Ukrainians with 73% of the vote. He soon turned out to be a ruthless tyrant and racist. Anyone who speaks Russian was quickly regarded as noncitizens, and those are the inhabitants of the two self-proclaimed states. In 2015, the Minsk Accords were drawn up, promising Donetsk and Luhansk far-reaching autonomy, plus elections about their future status in Ukraine. But Zelensky wants to force the two states into absolute obedience. He oppresses the Russian-speaking people, he disregards the Minsk agreements and he increases tensions with Russia, much to the delight of the NATO countries that are out for WWIII.

Putin warns Kiev to stop all military actions against these two people's republics, which are about to end in genocide or there will be crackdowns. Putin does not see Ukraine as an independent state, but as a vassal of the west with a puppet government. It is clear to the Kremlin that Ukraine is stirring up emotions and provoking a confrontation. The West threatens economic sanctions, such as cutting Russia off from the SWIFT system. Putin threatens to cut gas supplies to Europe.

Anyway, Russia and the West are facing each other with drawn knives. There is some growling, the teeth are bared and the hair on the neck is straight. According to Xander News, the west's sole aim is to cut Europe off from cheap Russian gas, which will result in skyrocketing gas and electricity prices. According to Xander News, the west cannot win a war with Russia. Russian army vehicles carrying state-of-the-art S-550 anti-aircraft missiles have been sighted near the border with Poland. These can destroy satellites and ballistic missiles. Without satellites, it is difficult for NATO's to see what is happening on the battlefield and all communications will fail. In the event of a ground war, the West is bound to lose because they have cut back on heavy artillery in favor of stealth aircraft. If the West were to unleash its nuclear submarines on Russia, which is not to be hoped, Russia will undoubtedly retaliate in the same way. That would immediately mean the end of Western society. I don't think you can even dream of a build back better then. It is also worth mentioning that, according to Xander News, Putin is not one of Schwab's Global Young Leaders. On this site you can read why and who has participated with Schwab since 1993: https://www.anti-spiegel.ru/2021/war-putin-ein-young-global-leader-von-klaus-schwab-die- schwarmintelligenz-liefert-eindeutige-antwort/. It is striking that Verhofstadt does appear in these lists. And then we read in arnowellens.eu that Verhofstad will speak about the future of Europe on 22/2/22 in the House of Representatives in The Hague. It will be about migration, digitization, values and youth issues. I think this needs no further explanation.

22/2/22 is also the day we hear that the occupation of Ottawa by the Canadian Truckers has come to an end. Their money was blocked, they were arrested, their vehicles were seized and they were forcibly driven from the city. So they lost this round, but whether they will lose the war remains to be seen. Canadians are more determined than ever to end tyranny. They agree to stop supplying Ottawa. In addition, the Prime Ministers of Alberta and six other provinces are suing Trudeau and his government for illegally enacting the Emergencies Act.

We are now 24/2/22 and we read in Xander News that Putin is launching a defensive military operation against bases and positions of the Ukrainian army. He is demilitarizing and de-nazifying Ukraine. In doing so, he is responding to the requests for help from the Russian-speaking people of the republics in the Donbass. Explosions and gunfights are reported on military targets where a huge number of NATO aircraft loaded with weapons have recently landed. In retrospect, we learn that the lying media uses old images of gunfights in Syria and an explosion in China from 2015. I also read that the Russian military units are meeting little resistance and that a few dozen Ukrainian soldiers are defecting to the Russian army. The gas supplies to the West continue, with which Putin indicates that he wants to leave European citizens undisturbed. He only wants to restore peace and rid Ukraine of the Western neo-Nazi puppet regime and punish those who committed crimes against humanity.

According to some reports on Telegram, Putin would drain the swamp there. Because Ukraine is said to be the cradle of human trafficking, organ trafficking and drug trafficking. On several telegram pages I read that the American soldiers are resigning en masse from the army. I also learn via Telegram that bio-warfare labs, where amplified viruses are made, are being seized in Kiev. According to Xander News of 26/2/22, very dangerous pathogens that cause smallpox have been bred. It's the variola virus. This infects the lungs and the death rates could rise to over eighty percent. Experimentation with this virus is banned worldwide and attempts to do something with it are crimes against peace and against humanity. Now, in these labs, they would have managed to give this variola virus the structure of a coronavirus, thus disguising it. The Russians found out. Furthermore, CNN is re-enacting the same man allegedly executed by the Taliban in Afghanistan as the first American victim of the "Ukraine crisis."

Niburu of 24/2/22 reports that the Ukrainian Air Force has since been shut down, so that they no longer pose a threat to the inhabitants of the republics in the east. Kiev screams bloody murder and claims that Putin has started his invasion. But Putin has no intention of conquering Ukraine. He wants to punish the NATO-backed neo-Nazis in Kiev, who have been in charge and have been attacking civilian targets in the east of the country for eight years. Putin also emphasizes that for thirty years he has tried unsuccessfully to negotiate with NATO to prevent it from expanding eastwards. And that despite the fact that after WWII Russia received a promise from the Americans that NATO would never expand further east than the eastern border with Germany.

And yet another message on Telegram refers to a speech by Putin in which he says he is not fighting against Ukraine but against the NWO. I watch the YouTube video and indeed I come to the conclusion that it is correct. Putin exposes all the lies and malpractice of the deceitful West. He comes to the conclusion, to put it in my own words, that there is no negotiating with the Schwab guys. He calls them contrary to human nature. He also warns any potential aggressor that Russia will strike hard if necessary. He does not tolerate NATO installations and NATO troops near Russia's borders and after thirty years of fruitless palaver with people you cannot talk to, he has had enough. Because while there is senseless talk, NATO's are moving their arsenals ever closer to the Russian border. Now the red line has been crossed.

Then he talks about the situation in Donbass. For eight years he has tried to resolve matters in a political way. It was no longer to be seen, there was a genocide going on on people, who hoped to one day be part of Russia again. In addition, Ukraine wanted to have nuclear weapons and that is unacceptable. He also says that he respects the sovereignty of all states that were formerly part of Russia. He only asks that Russian sovereignty will be respected as well. Russia will never attack a country that is peace-loving towards Russia. Russia does claim the right to defend its borders. During his speech he regularly refers to UN treaties and agreements, which were not violated by him, but by the West, and which he only defends.

He then addresses the people of Ukraine. His intention is not to annex Ukraine, but he does ask that they understand what is going on and that they work with Russia so that this tragic page in history can be quickly turned around and that they can move on as friendly and independent states.

He also addresses the Ukrainian army and points out how their grandfathers and great-grandfathers fought against the Nazi occupiers. The Nazis were also expelled from Ukraine. You swore an oath to serve the people and not looters and murderers, Putin says, asking them to lay down their arms and go home. He places all responsibility for potential bloodshed with the ruling Ukrainian regime.

Then Putin notifies those who would like to intervene from outside. Anyone who dares to stand in the way of Russian military actions will face immediate consequences unprecedented in history. They are ready.

Then he has another word for the Russian people. He appeals to their patriotism and asks them to maintain social cohesion and to adapt quickly to changes if necessary. He asks them to brace themselves and be strong, for they are at war with an "empire of lies". I understand that the time for talking is over and that the Russians, if necessary, will sell their lives dearly. At least Russia has truth and justice on its side and that makes them strong, he says. I must admit that my knowledge of discernment throughout this speech has not noticed any red flags.

In Xander News of 25/2/22 we read that behind its hypocritical harsh denunciations towards Kremlin, the West now has its desired scapegoat to blow up its own economy and take a big step towards the great-reset climate dictatorship of the WEF. The Russian army crushes the Ukrainian army, eliminates military targets and spares the cities and civilian population, except Kiev, the headquarters of the clown Zelensky who, along with the Cabal puppets of the West, brought the world to the brink of a world war. The psychopath Zelensky doesn't shy away from using his own citizens as human shields and even shooting at them, afterwards he blames the Russians for killing civilians, and the Mockingbird press reports it. The mainstream media also states about large amounts of war equipment that the West is sending to Ukraine. That means that Europe is actively participating in a war that doesn't concern them and that military retaliation from Russia may follow. Moreover, this extra military material slows down the advance of the Russians and that the extra armor can turn a guerrilla war against the Russians into a very long conflict.

On 27/2/22 we read in Xander News about the top economist Armstrong who sees the arms supplies to Ukraine as a declaration of war. Putin has put his weapons of mass destruction in deterrent mode so that the threat of nuclear war becomes very real. If Russia and China work together, the West, which is fully destroying itself in the context of the Great Reset, will be done in no time. Armstrong points out that the war strategy of the Russians is very different from that of the Americans. When the Americans invade, they destroy everything with heavy artillery. That costs billions in help to rebuild everything and you make the survivors into sworn enemies. Putin wants to install a new government with as few civilian casualties as possible. He has surrounded the cities and is waiting for the people to surrender. That way you keep everything intact. He takes soldiers prisoner, as soon as there is a new government, they become allies. We also read that only thirty percent of Russian troops have crossed the border into Ukraine. The rest are ready to take Europe, if EU leaders were stupid enough to interfere Manu Militari.

Armstrong calls Putin a strategist. He plays chess and is very good at it. In 2013, he avoided WWIII for Syria. The Russian military intervened and the US (Obama), Turkey and Saudi Arabia created and controlled IS, intended to overthrow ASAD, was stopped and defeated. Now, the West's meddling in Ukraine has jeopardized its post-war security structure and Putin has put its defensive nuclear weapons on standby.

The strategy of the fascist tyrant Zelensky is to arm the civilians and let them fight against trained soldiers. He wants to see blood and he makes many innocent victims to feed the Western media in order to persuade NATO to actively participate in the war. The Mockingbird press is already doing its best to demonize Putin and the Russians. And meanwhile, China makes a sudden turn towards North Korea.

On 28/2/22 we learned via nos.nl that the peace talks between Russia and Ukraine have ended. The diplomats return to Moscow and Kiev to consult their governments. The meeting will resume in a few days. Belarus supports the Kremlin and allows Russia to plant nuclear weapons on its territory. Zelenski wants to join the EU quickly, but he gets the answer that this is possible in the long run (somewhere in the distant future). Procedures must be followed. These procedures are complex and can take years. The ties with Ukraine can be further strengthened. Gullible and media-brain-washed Westerners deposit money and collect relief supplies for the people in thoroughly corrupt Ukraine, where the sons of the Cabal friends have beautiful and well-paid posts in the energy sector. Just think of Hunter Biden, Paul Pelosi Jr., son of Nancy Pelosi, and the son of former Secretary of State John Kerry and former Senator Mitt Romney. (Source: apokalypsnu.nl).

March:

Ukraine panic replaces corona panic

Apparently Corona is no longer the enemy we all have to fight. Now it's the Russians again.

As for the escalation in Ukraine, I think it's good to provide some geo-political background. To start, we listen to a YouTube video from 9/25/2015 from the University of Chicago, where Prof. John Mearsheimer has the floor. The title is "Why is Ukraine the West's fault". The video lasts about 75 minutes and has 13,116,550 views. Mearsheimer first outlines a background to the crisis. I summarize it all in my own words and supplement it with information from Wikipedia, Xander Nieuws and vrijspreker.nl.

Ukraine is divided between the western part where the inhabitants speak Ukrainian and the eastern part where Russian is spoken. The people of the west want to be part of the EU, those of the east want to be part of Russia. Yet there is a kind of balance and because Europe is dependent on Russian gas and oil, the EU keeps its ease and that allows Russia to have political influence in Ukraine.

Now there are several causes for the crisis in Ukraine. There is the structural cause, the impetus, the Russian reaction and the West's meddling with the Orange Revolution.

The deeper, structural reason is that the US and its European allies want to take Ukraine out of the Russian sphere of influence and incorporate it into the West. Then Ukraine, which is by far the largest country in Europe, would become a Western stronghold, right next to Russia. That makes the West responsible for the chaos. Because Russia obviously does not agree and says it will do everything it can to prevent this. Yet despite promises made to Russia before, the West wants an expansion of NATO and an expansion of the EU and they are advancing towards the Russian border. Meanwhile, the Eastern bloc has already been annexed to the EU (economically) and NATO (militarily). However, these countries do not border Russia. Now they also want to take over Ukraine economically and militarily, while that is an absolute no-go for Russia, because then the EU and NATO will be on top of the Russian border.

In order to achieve their goal, the West set out to instigate the Orange Revolution. I.e. that they became involved in the popular uprisings, which started spontaneously from 22/11/2004 after the second round of the presidential elections and threatened to split the country in two. The election campaign took place in a heated atmosphere, characterized by intimidation, violence, media manipulation and mutual accusations.

Until then, the dictator Kuchma was in power. His politics was focused on Russia and he was mainly the president of the big industrialists, the oligarchs. Yanukovych , who also took a pro-Russian stance, won the election by a narrow majority. His counterpart Yushchenko, who was oriented more to the west, and his supporters claimed that there was fraud in the elections. Europe got involved in the elections and eventually a third round of elections took place on 26/12 where the pro-Western Yushchenko won with a large majority. The elections were fair, according to about 12,000 international observers from 44 countries. Now Yanukovych alleges fraud and threatens to challenge his defeat in the Ukrainian Supreme Court. But his charge was dismissed.

If we delve deeper into history, we learn that Ukraine was part of the Soviet Union for 70 years. The Ukrainians had a hard time, then. In the 1930s, Stalin deliberately starved the Ukrainian population by forcibly taking their grain and other crops and exporting them abroad for financial gain. More people died in this oft-forgotten "Holodomor" than in the Holocaust. This also meant that during WWII the Ukrainians welcomed the Germans. They hoped that the Nazi regime would be a little more bearable than living under the yoke of Stalin, but that turned out to be a vain hope. After WWII, Ukraine rejoined the U.S.S.R.

In the 1990s and 2000s, NATO expanded rapidly eastwards. Only Ukraine remained an ally of Russia. In 2004 the orange revolution took place with the support of the West. The elections were declared invalid and a more pro-Western president came to power. This was not very successful and after a few years Yanukovych returned to power. He did become prime minister between 2006 and 2007, and he became president from 2010 to 2014. He was a president who had close ties to business and his political agenda included decentralization, government subsidies for the ailing industries and a good social safety net. He gave a lot of support to the east, where the Russian-speaking people live. His tone was anti-nationalist, anti-Western and pro-Russian.

The direct cause that led to the coup of 22/2/2014 is that on 21/11/2013 President Yanukovych rejected the association agreement with the EU because Russia had a better proposal. This gave rise to large demonstrations, strikes, occupations, in short, a popular uprising. Many Ukrainians were frustrated by the corruption and economic stagnation under Yanukovych's sway. The Western powers made good use of this to achieve their political goals. They further incited the Ukrainian population through the media. Some Western politicians, including Guy Verhofstad, went to Ukraine to cheer on the protesting crowds. On 18/2/2014, the protesters were shot. This shooting was orchestrated by the West. A secret unit was dropped with orders to shoot at both the protesters and the police. At the end, the West got its way. Yanukovych was accused of mass murder and fled to Russia. The next day, parliament voted to repeal the language laws of the Russian-speaking people. In response, Russia, with the consent of the people, annexed Crimea. For the West, this was an illegal annexation. Then the uprisings in eastern Ukraine began, led by pro-Russian elements, because they, too, preferred to belong to Russia. These separatists were supported by Moscow. What followed was a civil war that was tearing the country apart, the economy stagnated and inflation spiraled out of control.

Putin gives an ultimatum to the West. Either they freeze the conflict and make Ukraine a buffer state, or Russia destroys Ukraine. But the West, which never admits its mistakes, is getting tougher because they think Russia wants to expand its territory (talking about a projection). Economic sanctions are being introduced against Russia. A la limite, the West is making a big mouth of it, while it is dependent on Russian gas and oil. You should also keep in mind that Russia is a nuclear power and that they will only use their nuclear weapons if they come under extreme pressure and feel that their survival is at stake. So if you go to challenge Russia, you risk a third world war. The West should therefore carefully consider whether they want Ukraine, which is not at all of vital strategic importance to the West (it is to Russia), to join the EU and NATO.

According to Mearsheimer, the solution is to make Ukraine a neutral buffer state between the NATO countries and Russia. So that takes you back to the status quo. That's how you keep the peace, he says. You do not do that by dividing Ukraine into a western part that belongs to the EU and an eastern part that belongs to Russia. In addition, you should give the minorities in Ukraine sufficient rights and freedoms, such as the right to speak their own language and the right to choose their own representatives. That was also the case in the Minsk agreements, which were tossed in the trash by Kiev with the approval of the West. Ultimately, that was Putin's proposal in 2013, and the EU declined. By intensifying the conflict with Russia, you drive Russia into the arms of China, says Mearsheimer, and that is exactly what we are experiencing now, in 2022. That is not smart, because it is better to have Russia as an ally.

What follows comes from Sputnik International. There it is written that Russia is conducting this special operation to protect the people's republics of Donets and Luhansk. The West is screaming bloody murder, while for years it has turned a blind eye to the crimes committed by the Ukrainian army against Donbass. This army includes the Azov Regiment, an openly neo-Nazi unit operating within the National Guard that adopts Swastika-style runic insignia. The Azov regiment also houses neo-Nazi volunteers from countries such as Sweden, Italy, Russia, France, Belarus, Canada and Slovenia. Then there is the Right Sector, a hard-hitting nationalist paramilitary union turned political party and striving for a nationalist Ukrainian state. Members of this group are notorious for their atrocities. The Right Sector argued strongly for a strong solution to the Donbass crisis and rejected the negotiated approach.

According to a recent statement by the Commission of Inquiry of the Russian Federation, both are accused of complicity in crimes against humanity committed in Donbass, eastern Ukraine. This has been going on for eight years now, since the coup in Kiev in 2014, which was co-instigated by the West. They hope to bring more than 400 criminal cases to court, as 2,600 civilians have been killed and more than 5,500 injured in Donbass. The charges include kidnapping, torture, use of banned substances and methods of war.

The continuation of the Russian military operation in Ukraine can be read in Xander News of 2/3/22. It is sneered at the Telegraaf, in which it is written that the corona wappies are often Putin fans. Well, in the meantime we also know where the real thinkers are and that is not in the camp of the WEF and the NWO, with their Mockinbird gazettes. And we also read that it is only to be hoped that Putin wins and that he does not press the red button in utter despair. In that respect we are in good shape, because the Russian army has meanwhile liberated the south-eastern half of Ukraine, where the Russian-speaking people live.

Furthermore, I get the following information from Sputnik International. On 3/3/22, Russian and Ukrainian delegations held a second round of talks in Belarus. They agreed to jointly organize humanitarian corridors to ensure the evacuation of civilians and the supply of food and medicine. They will continue the negotiations as soon as possible. The second week of the special military operation is now underway and everything is going according to plan.

The West is actively participating in this war by sending war materials and mercenaries into the "war zone". Unlike the Ukrainian soldiers and the mercenaries, who use the civilians as human shields, the Russian soldiers strive to inflict as few civilian casualties as possible.

Niburu of 4/3/22 talks about the "comedian" Zelensky, who does everything in his power to cause panic and start a WWIII. Russian troops captured the Zaporizhzhya nuclear power plant last night. Zelensky felt it necessary to inform the world that Russian tanks fired at the nuclear power plant, that a fire broke out and that increased radiation has been observed. There was a fire in the training complex next door, as a result of the shelling, and it was quickly extinguished. As a result, U.S. Senator Lindsey Graham made an icy appeal to assassinate Putin. In the mainstream press we read that the leader of Germany's largest opposition party, Friedrich Merz of the CDU/CSU, believes that NATO will have to decide at some point to intervene and stop Putin. Because it is unacceptable that the Russians target nuclear power plants. British Prime Minister Boris Johnson talks about reckless actions that threaten the security of all of Europe. Anyway, Biden, Trudeau, Draghi and Payne are concerned and are calling for unity and determined action.

Wim Turkenburg, nuclear energy expert and emeritus professor at Utrecht University, says there is no threat to Europe. Moscow did not want to destroy the plant, but did want to control it. The Russians now operate the energy supply in the region. Besides, if they were to bomb a nuclear power plant, that would also endanger Russia itself. They're not that stupid. Meanwhile, more than a million refugees from Ukraine are on their way to the West.

The corona plandemic is in its final convulsions and the shares of Pfizer and Moderne are plummeting. On 5/3/22, the Vaccinvrij Foundation shares the following information. Moderna is down 70 percent from its peak and Pfizer is down 19 percent. Former BlackRock portfolio manager and investment advisor Edward Dowd says Moderna will drop to zero and Pfizer to below $10 a share. Dowd predicted the bursting of the dotcom bubble and he saw in time that the home mortgage rating system was corrupted. Now he is sounding the alarm about Pfizer and Moderna as sinking ships that savvy investors urgently need to abandon. Moreover, he expects a total collapse of the financial market as the debt bubble is about to burst. Under the cover of Covid, sixty-five percent more money has been printed to keep the system afloat for a while. We are at the end of the ride. Dowd thinks the emerging medical technocracy dictatorship under the guise of covid is serving to contain the masses as they realize the economy is collapsing, resulting in the loss of pensions and benefit income. Dowd also foresees an avalanche of lawsuits as the insurance industry continues to expose the many deaths from mRNA vaccines. Because vaccine makers can be held liable if there is fraud, and that is now the case. And finally, if you want to invest smartly, you should buy shares in funeral companies. Or, with the looming third world war, you could also invest in companies that make air-raid shelters. Because the rich of the EU buy massively luxurious doomsday bunkers, which cost several millions. The demand for it has increased by a thousand percent.

Code yellow will go into effect on 7/3/22 and the measures including the CST and the mouth mask obligation in Belgium will be abolished. This will also happen in France next week. However, the green light has been given for the booster dose for 12-17 year olds. The "vaxxide" continues unimpeded as the conflict in Ukraine distracts all attention.

Xander News of 7/3/22 headlines: "New pandemic treaty gives WHO all power, mandatory vaccinations from October this year." From May 2022, WHO will have full power over all 194 member states, not just in the event of a pandemic, but in the event of any disaster or threat. The EU is working hard towards a mandatory European QR-ID vax pass this summer. The intention is to continuously boost people. Anyone who refuses the booster will be considered unvaccinated and will no longer receive medical care or access to their bank account.

On 7/3/22 there is also a YouTube video on apokalypsnu.nl, where Karel van Wolferen, editor of "Gezond Verstand" (common sense) is interviewed. The title is, Ukraine: The Front of the Information War. According to van Wolferen, Zelenski belongs to the Schwab clique and Putin certainly does not. Putin is not an autocrat. He must take into account groups that would rather unite with Europe and America. Medvedev used to be there too. Today Medvedev stands behind Putin. Then there is the fifth column, which wants to make Russia fail from within. Industries, ores, raw materials, art, etc. have been systematically looted by the oligarchs together with Western authorities. Putin didn't want that. When he succeeded Yeltsin in late 1999, he opposed further division of the Russian Federation. He succeeded and that is why he has the support of the people.

Militarily, Russia is far ahead of America. But if the West puts its nuclear warheads close to the border, you get a different story. Then the US can conquer Russia with a so-called 'first strike'. Now a nuclear propaganda bomb has been unleashed over Europe and the US, driving all heads of government completely mad. They put Putin in a bad light, while they have no idea what is really going on. Demonizing Putin has been part of the prescribed narrative for much longer, and it is an outright lie. As a result, Canadian truckers, for example, are now holding hands with their policymakers and waving Ukrainian flags while protesting against Russia. Everyone suddenly sympathizes with Ukraine. Russian composers are banned, as are Russian sports people, Russian vodka is flushed down the sink and everything Russian is suddenly taboo. If you want to be on the right side, you're on Zelensky's side and that is the result of years of NATO/EU/US indoctrination, which the media has worked hard to bring about.

Schwab and his followers want to install a technocratic tyranny, which does not take into account changes, parameters and suddenly emerging problems. They do not assume an ever-changing and evolving reality. They think they know everything in advance and can come up with solutions for everything. They fail to see and tackle the obstacles that suddenly arise, because that requires a holistic view. In a technocracy, all specialists, experts, professors, politicians, etc. work side by side without knowing what the other is doing and what is really going on. They are all in a bubble that is hermetically sealed from reality. That makes them life-threatening. From that bubble they want to organize reality in such a way that they have total control over it. This must be done via that QR passport, which must be issued from 1/7/22. The strategist Putin is in touch with reality and he keeps that overview.

Here, the press provides information about the war in Ukraine based on what they know about US warfare, which often involved NATO member states, in Iraq, Afghanistan, Libya, Serbia, etc. That is a strategy of shock and hold. Collateral damage is not taken into account and a trail of destruction is left behind. Putin works differently. He is still not in Kiev. So the West thinks he's losing. But Putin doesn't want innocent victims.

The civilian population is not the enemy, he says. They are victims of the 2014 coup d'état, however, he has eliminated the main military hubs, in particular the air and naval forces, in one fell swoop and with precision. Subsequently, the Russian military quickly spread across the country with small units cutting off communication between the commandos and the field armies. The soldiers thus cut off from their commanders are allowed to go home if they surrender. Apparently that happens en masse.

NATO countries supply weapons and volunteers via Poland. This is punishable, because it goes against all UN conventions. They think they can get away with it. But meanwhile, the UN is losing even more credibility. They think that unity in the West is stronger than ever and it will soon be just the opposite.

In Poland and Romania there are NATO missiles that you can equip with nuclear warheads. This means that the West has reached a first strike capacity. Russia then has no choice but to also unpack with nuclear weapons, so that you scare off the fools who call themselves leaders in the West by showing what you can do. The great leader of the West is demented and underneath there is a vacuum that has been filled of late by neo-conservatives (Bush-minded).

After the coup, which in the West is called a popular uprising, crimes against the Russian-speaking inhabitants began. It was necessary to take back Crimea immediately. Things were also very bad in Donetsk and Luhansk. In the middle area you have a population that speaks part Ukrainian and part Russian. After the coup, only Ukrainian was allowed to be spoken on TV and politics had to be conducted in Ukrainian. That created resistance in Donetsk and Luhansk. There is now heavy fighting. The Azov battalion was already preparing a massacre there. 40,000 Russian-speaking Ukrainians had already been killed there. That means that Russia had no choice but to intervene. In addition, Zelensky wanted nuclear weapons. They would have literally stood on the Russian border. Putin has prevented a serious disaster here, which would have resulted in an enormous number of victims. He also captured Europe's largest nuclear power plant before Zelensky committed a nuclear disaster.

The predecessors of the Nazi Azov battalion fought with Hitler against Russia at the time. Stalin starved 16 million Ukrainians in the 1950s. Other sources (armstrongeconomics.com speak of seven million). The hatred of the Ukrainians against Russia and the Russian-speaking people is very deep. In addition to the Azov battalion, Western (CIA) paid mercenaries fight. Ukrainians are currently dying and that is due to the policies of the Ukrainian government. Kalashnikovs are distributed in Kiev. Criminals have been released from prison to fight. The government teaches them how to make Molotov cocktails. People are already shooting at each other. Citizens have sold their Kalashnikov on the black market, then they have something left over, because despite the fact that Ukraine is the breadbasket of Europe, the inhabitants have never had a good time.

The Azov commando is now surrounded in Mariupol. No more food and drink comes in and they wait for them to give up. The Russians expect that those Nazis will not surrender, the alternative is that they fight to the death. Corridors have been built so that the civilians can get out, but those who flee are executed on the spot by the soldiers of the Ukrainian checkpoints. Entire families are shot there. The corridors are also strewn with mines, in order to kill as many civilians as possible and put the blame on Putin. The question is whether this will ever appear in the mainstream press. The Mockingbird media obviously blame the Russian military for the civilian casualties.

According to van Wolferen, covid will not come back. After Russia we will have to deal with the climate hoax, with the gas of life, CO_2 as a new enemy. And that while the lung of Europe, the Carpathian forest was being cut down. In addition, a shortage of CO_2 will lead to a catastrophic cooling of the earth.

On 9/3/22 we read in Xander News that more and more countries are starting to see how the West is endangering all of humanity. The huge price increases of energy, food, and many products would have been completely unnecessary if Ukraine had simply respected the Minsk agreements and given the people of Donbass a voice over their future. But the Western globalists need a crisis to push through their worldwide WEF/WHO climate dictatorship, also called their Fourth Reich (4IR). For that, they have brought humanity to the brink of WWIII. A war predicted by Armstrong's computers.

The leaders of Saudi Arabia and the United Arab Emirates do not want to take the call from Biden, on his knees, pleading for oil and gas. Under no circumstances will they produce more oil. Meanwhile, the West continues to boycott the Russian economy by no longer buying oil, gas and coal, because that is how the Russian war chest is sponsored. Europe imports 45% of its coal needs from Russia, 40% of its gas needs and 27% of its oil. The European economy in particular relies on these fossil fuels. Niburu of 9/3/22 warns of an energy shortage and a planned energy lockdown, which will further wreck our economy. You could say that the Great Reset has erupted in full force.

The Xander News see Putin as a WEF dissident who must rid the world of the Western Empire of Lies. The Russian army would then be the last bastion against the satanic New World Order. And we now know what the task of Russia is, in terms of human development. I wonder if Putin also knows that.

End

Printed in Great Britain
by Amazon